W9-AMR-579

BACON COOKBOOK

Quick & Easy Recipes

Bonnie Scott

Copyright © 2015 Bonnie Scott

All rights reserved.

ISBN-13: 978-1507872956

Contents

Bacon Introduction

Young, old, rich, poor, thin or not-so-slim, almost everyone loves bacon. The meaty, smoky aroma as it's cooking, the rich, salty taste and the unmistakable sizzle as it's frying in the pan are memories we all share and savor. Whether standard fare for breakfast, a decadent topping for a burger or a crunchy addition to a favorite salad, bacon is at home with any meal. With the latest surge in bacon-love, you'll even see quite a few desserts that call for bacon.

For a number of years, bacon had been the black sheep of the pork industry. With its high fat content and the recommendation that nitrates are bad for one's health, bacon consumption shriveled. However, bacon is one of those things you should indulge in. You shouldn't eat it too often, nor do you need to make an entire meal of it – as enticing as that may sound. But when you want to treat yourself, there's nothing that satisfies like the savory, crunchy goodness of bacon.

Bacon has come in and out of favor over the past few decades, and it's currently one of the hottest food trends around – encompassing every course on the menu from appetizers to beverages and desserts. Because of this renewed interest in the humble pork belly, this cookbook has a host of recipes that feature bacon as either a main ingredient or as a flavor enhancer.

You'll find a wealth of tips, advice and more recipes than you've ever thought of in this tribute to one of the favorite and most beloved meats in our culture. So, sit back and enjoy browsing through the pages of The Bacon Cookbook.

Bacon Aficionado Tips And Tricks

Take your bacon expertise to the next culinary level with this handy guide of bacon tips for storing, preparing and using your favorite pork product.

Pan Frying Bacon – Use medium heat to fry bacon. A heavy cast iron or stainless skillet ensures the heat is distributed evenly over the bottom of the pan. A thin-bottomed skillet may have hot spots and cause some areas of your bacon to burn while other portions remain limp.

Don't neglect your bacon! It's very easy to overcook and burn bacon, so don't wander away while it's cooking. You'll also need to move the strips around and turn them over at least once. You don't need a high heat to cook your bacon to a tasty crispness. Just allow the medium heat and a little extra time to turn your limp strips into crunchy goodness.

Baking Bacon – If you're in need of a lot of bacon, this method allows you to make it all at once. As a bonus, you don't need to continually monitor it, so you can go on with other chores. You also won't wind up with grease covering every nook and cranny of your stove.

Preheat your oven to 400 degrees Fahrenheit and line a large broiler pan with aluminum foil. Face the shiny side of the foil down. Place a rack in the pan, position your bacon on the rack so they don't touch and place on the center rack of the oven. Depending on how crisp you want your bacon and how thick it is, it will take between 11 to 15 minutes. Rotate the pan halfway through the baking process, so all the bacon cooks evenly. Use tongs to remove the bacon and drain on a paper towel lined plate. Be sure to save those bacon drippings! Allow the drippings to cool somewhat and fold up the aluminum to form a funnel to pour off the drippings into a container.

If you want to use the oven for other recipes at the same time, you can use a lower temperature. However, you're increasing the baking time considerably.

Broiling Bacon – You can broil the bacon by placing it on a rack three inches beneath the flame. Turn it once while cooking and keep a close eye on it. The amount of time depends a lot on the thickness of the bacon.

Microwaving Bacon – This technique is especially good for cooking a small amount of bacon, and leaves very little clean-up. Place four or five strips of bacon between a couple layers of paper toweling on a microwave-safe plate.

Depending on the power of your microwave, cook the strips about 45 seconds to one minute per strip on full power. This should be no more than about 5 minutes. If the bacon isn't crispy enough, add an additional 30 to 60 seconds to get it to your favorite crunchiness.

Preparing Bacon Bits – In theory you can stack up your bacon strips and cut them into bite-size strips or diced pieces with your knife. But if you don't have a really, really sharp knife and very cold bacon, you may tend to demolish those little strips into a mushy mess of stringy fat and bits of meat.

Keep a pair of good, stainless steel scissors in your kitchen for food preparation. They're great to cut up bacon into neat, uniform bites. Stack up a few strips of bacon and simply snip them into the size you need. You'll find tons of uses for your kitchen shears – just keep them hidden from the rest of the family!

Refrigerating Bacon – Bacon is one of those staples that has a long shelf life in your frig. It may have an expiration date of several weeks or a month from the day you purchase it. However, once you've opened the package, you should use it in about a week.

Freezing Bacon – You can easily freeze bacon just as it comes in its original packaging. However, if you can't see yourself using a whole pound of bacon quickly, you can separate the strips into usable portions, wrap them in plastic wrap and tuck in your freezer. Some folks say that the meat changes taste after six to eight weeks, while others claim to freeze it much longer with no loss of flavor. You can also freeze cooked bacon, but you shouldn't let it sit in the freezer more than a few weeks.

Cut Down On Grease Splatters – Add just enough water to cover the bottom of a skillet before adding the bacon. Turn the stove to high and cook until the water has evaporated. Now, turn down the heat to medium and continue to cook until crisp. Surprisingly, this works!

Use Your Countertop Grill – if you have a Foreman grill or an electric Panini maker, put the bacon strips in and save cleaning the stovetop. You also free up the burners for cooking other items.

Bacon Goes Great In So Many Dishes!

Add crumbled or diced bacon to perk up the flavor quotient of your family's favorite recipes. Here are a few tips to get you started:

- Sprinkle bacon bits over grilled vegetables and toss just before serving.

- Punch up plain cooked vegetables. Use bacon drippings to sauté minced garlic, shallots or onion until fragrant. Add diced, cooked bacon and your favorite cooked vegetable. Goes great with beans, summer squash, broccoli, Brussel sprouts and many other veggies.

- Diced bacon adds another layer of flavor to pancakes. Put fried bacon right in the batter to have bacon in every bite of your pancakes.

- Add crumbled bacon to your potato salad. You can also use bacon drippings as a substitution for part of the mayonnaise or dressing. You can even add it to deli or prepackaged salads. It gives a homemade touch to your store-bought side dish.

- Diced bacon in chicken salad adds a lot of flavor to a somewhat bland sandwich filling.

- Creamed spinach gets a pick-me-up when you add some diced bacon to the dish and use bacon drippings to make the cream sauce.

- Coat both sides of your bacon with flour before frying it. The flour minimizes the grease spitting, minimizes shrinkage and who doesn't love crusty fried anything?

- Bacon drippings make great cream gravy. Make a roux to thicken and use evaporated milk for tasty gravy that's great on biscuits, cornbread or thick slices of hearty bread.

- Use bacon drippings in place of oil to prepare popcorn.

- Bacon drippings are great for coating Idaho potatoes before baking them.

- If you make your own refried beans, use bacon drippings instead of lard.

- Pour cool bacon drippings into an ice tray and place in freezer. When cubes are frozen, pop them out of the tray and seal in a freezer storage bag. You'll have fresh bacon drippings whenever the mood strikes.

- Cooking anything in bacon drippings adds so much flavor. Use part peanut oil and part bacon drippings when frying chicken. Fried eggs are the absolute best when cooked in bacon drippings. For you die-hard liver and onion fans, use bacon drippings to add extra flavor to that special dish.

Snacks, Appetizers

"Bring-Home-the-Bacon" Avocado Dip

2 ripe avocados, peeled and mashed
1/2 cup mayonnaise
1/4 cup onion, finely chopped
2 tablespoons lime juice
1/2 teaspoon salt
1/8 teaspoon hot sauce
5 slices bacon, crisply cooked and crumbled

Combine avocados, mayonnaise, onion, lime juice, salt and hot sauce in a small bowl; cover and refrigerate up to 2 hours. Stir in bacon. Serve with tortilla chips.

Yield: 2 cups.

Candied Bacon Appetizer

1 lb. bacon, cut each slice in thirds
1 cup brown sugar
1 teaspoon dry mustard

Line jelly roll pan with aluminum foil. Place single layer of bacon pieces on foil. Combine sugar and mustard; scatter on bacon, and bake in preheated oven at 275 degrees F for 1 hour. Drain bacon drippings from pan and place bacon on brown paper to drain. Can be served hot or cold.

Stuffed Jalapenos

24 fresh whole jalapenos, halved lengthwise and seeded
2 (8 oz.) packages cream cheese
1 teaspoon garlic
1 teaspoon chili powder
1/2 cup bacon, cooked crisp and crumbled
1 (8 oz.) package shredded Cheddar cheese

Cut jalapenos lengthwise and clean out. Combine cream cheese, garlic, chili powder, bacon and cheese; fill jalapenos. Bake at 300 degrees F for 45 minutes.

Bacon 'N Egg Dip

1 (6 oz.) can tomato paste
1/2 cup mayonnaise or salad dressing
3 hard-boiled eggs, quartered
10 slices bacon, cooked crisp and crumbled
1/4 medium green bell pepper, cut into 1 inch squares
1/4 teaspoon salt
1/8 teaspoon pepper
1/8 teaspoon hot red pepper sauce

Combine all ingredients in a blender container. Blend until smooth, stopping motor and scraping down sides as needed. Serve with crisp crackers or melba toast.

Yield: 2 cups.

Bacon Popcorn Salad

6 cups popped corn
6 to 8 slices bacon, crisply cooked and crumbled
1 (5 oz.) can water chestnuts, drained
1 cup mayonnaise
1 cup shredded Cheddar cheese
1/2 cup sugar
1/2 cup celery
1/2 cup onion, diced

In a large bowl, combine bacon, water chestnuts, mayonnaise, cheese, sugar, celery and onion. Add popcorn just before serving, stirring to coat.

Zesty Bacon Dip

1 (8 oz.) carton sour cream
6 slices bacon, crisply cooked and crumbled
2 teaspoons prepared horseradish
1 teaspoon Worcestershire sauce

Combine all ingredients; cover and refrigerate at least 2 hours. Serve dip with pretzel chips.

Yield: 1 cup.

Cheesy Olive Appetizers

1 cup shredded Swiss cheese
6 slices bacon, cooked crisp and crumbled
1/4 cup chopped pimiento-stuffed olives
1/4 cup mayonnaise
2 tablespoons onion, chopped
20 slices party rye bread
Pimiento-stuffed olives, sliced

Combine cheese, bacon, olives, mayonnaise and onion; mix well. Spread one tablespoon cheese mixture on each slice of bread. Top each bread slice with a sliced olive. Broil 2 minutes or until cheese is melted; serve hot.

Yield: 20 servings.

Cheese Puffs

1 (4 oz.) tub whipped cream cheese
1 egg
1 teaspoon chives
1 teaspoon lemon juice
1/8 teaspoon black pepper
1/2 cup shredded sharp white Cheddar cheese
6 slices bacon, crisply cooked and crumbled
4 frozen patty or pastry shells, thawed

Stir together cream cheese, egg, chives, lemon juice and pepper; beat well. Add Cheddar cheese and bacon. Refrigerate. Roll one of the patty shells to 8 x 4" rectangle. Cut into 2 inch squares.

Top each square with a rounded teaspoon of filling. Brush edges with milk. Fold to form triangle; seal. Place on ungreased baking sheet. Repeat with remaining shells and filling. Refrigerate appetizers until ready to bake. Place in a preheated 450 degrees F oven. Immediately reduce temperature to 400 degrees F and bake 12 to 15 minutes.

Yield: 32 appetizers.

Bacon-Wrapped Water Chestnuts

1 lb. bacon
2 (8 oz.) cans whole water chestnuts
1 cup ketchup
1 cup brown sugar

Cut bacon into thirds and wrap a piece of bacon around each water chestnut. Hold together with toothpicks. Place in a 9x13x2" baking dish and bake in a preheated oven at 350 degrees F for 30 minutes. Drain grease. Combine brown sugar and ketchup; pour over water chestnuts. Return to oven and bake for 30 more minutes.

Pecan Stuffed Mushrooms

18 large fresh mushrooms
1/4 cup margarine (divided)
2 tablespoons vegetable oil
2 tablespoons onion, minced
5 slices bacon, crisply cooked and crumbled
1 cup soft bread crumbs
2 tablespoons pecans, chopped
2 tablespoons dry sherry
2 tablespoons sour cream
2 teaspoons chives, minced

Clean mushrooms. Remove stems and discard. Heat 2 tablespoons margarine and oil in large skillet. Add mushroom caps and sauté 3 minutes on each side. Remove caps, place on baking sheet. Melt 2 tablespoons margarine in skillet. Add onion and sauté until tender. Stir in bacon, bread crumbs, pecans, sherry, sour cream and chives. Spoon mixture into mushroom caps. Broil 5 inches from heat for 2 to 3 minutes.

Yield: 6 servings.

Hors D'Oeuvres

10 slices bacon, cooked crisp and crumbled (or 1 cup)
1 1/2 cups grated sharp cheese
1/4 cup onion, chopped
1 small loaf round party rye bread

Combine bacon, cheese and onion; spread on rye bread. Toast for 10 to 15 minutes on baking sheet at 350 degrees F or until heated through and cheese melts.

Cheese Roll

2 cups shredded Cheddar cheese
1/2 cup crumbled blue cheese
1 tablespoon onion, grated
1 tablespoon milk
1/2 teaspoon parsley
4 slices bacon, cooked crisp and crumbled
1 cup nuts, chopped

Beat Cheddar cheese, blue cheese and onion together until smooth; add milk. On waxed paper, roll cheese into a log, roll in bacon, nuts and parsley. Wrap in waxed paper and refrigerate. Before serving, bring to room temperature. Place on plate with crackers.

Yield: 1 1/2 cups.

Almond Stuffed Dates

1 lb. pitted dates
1 (4 oz.) package blanched whole almonds
1 1/4 lb. lean bacon slices

Stuff each date with an almond. Cut bacon slices into thirds and wrap a piece around each date; secure with a toothpick. Bake at 375 degrees F for 10 to 15 minutes until bacon is cooked but not brown. Drain on paper towels. Serve warm.

Festive Cheese and Bacon Dip

2 (8 oz.) packages cream cheese, softened and cut into cubes
4 cups shredded Colby-Jack cheese
1 cup half and half
1 tablespoon onion, chopped
2 tablespoons prepared mustard
2 teaspoons Worcestershire sauce
1/4 teaspoon hot pepper sauce
1/2 teaspoon salt
1 lb. bacon, cooked crisp and crumbled

Place all ingredients except bacon in a slow cooker. Stir together. Cover slow cooker and cook on low for 1 hour or until cheese is melted, stirring occasionally. Stir in bacon. Serve with crusty bread.

Rumaki

12 slices bacon
1/2 lb. chicken livers (about 6)
12 water chestnuts
3 tablespoons soy sauce
2 teaspoons sugar
1/8 teaspoon ground ginger
Toothpicks

Cut bacon strips in half and cook until partially cooked but still soft. Cut chicken livers into quarters. Slice the water chestnuts in half. In a bowl, combine soy sauce, sugar and ginger and add livers. Marinate for 20 minutes.

Wrap chicken livers and water chestnuts in the bacon strips and skewer in place with toothpicks. Place on a rack in a baking dish. Bake in preheated oven for 10 minutes at 450 degrees F. Replace toothpicks with fresh toothpicks before serving.

Bacon and Onion Spread

1 lb. bacon
6 green onions
5 tablespoons mayonnaise
4 English muffin halves

Cook bacon until crisp and then chop fine. Mince green onions and add to bacon, along with mayonnaise. Brown muffin halves; spread with bacon mixture. Toast in 350 degrees F oven for 10 minutes. Cut each half in quarters and serve.

Canadian Style Bacon Parfaits

6 slices (1/ 2" thick) Canadian style bacon
1 1/2 teaspoons prepared mustard
6 pineapple slices
6 cling peach halves
3 slices (4 x 7") mozzarella cheese, cut in half

Spread each slice of Canadian style bacon with 1/4 teaspoon mustard. Arrange slices of pineapple in baking pan. Place a slice of meat on each pineapple slice, and top with a peach half, cut side down. Arrange a half slice of cheese on each peach. Bake in preheated oven at 400 degrees F for 15 to 20 minutes, or until cheese is melted.

Bacon Stix

10 thin bread sticks
5 slices bacon, cut in half-lengthwise
1/2 cup Parmesan cheese, grated

Wrap a bacon strip around each bread stick like a maypole. Roll in the cheese. Place on a microwave rack lined with paper towels. Microwave on high 4 1/2 to 6 minutes, until the bacon is crisp. Roll again in cheese while still hot.

Serve at room temperature. If not using right away, keep refrigerated. They freeze well after baking and cooling. To double the yield and make smaller, cut in half before baking.

Yield: 10 bread sticks.

Sweet and Sour Dip

4 slices bacon, diced
1/4 cup bottled sweet & sour salad dressing
1 (8 oz.) package cream cheese, softened
2 tablespoons milk

In a small skillet, cook bacon until crisp; drain on paper towels and crumble. In a bowl, stir together salad dressing, cream cheese and milk; beat until smooth. Fold in bacon. Refrigerate for 2 or 3 hours; serve with fresh vegetables or crackers.

Bacon and Cheddar Dip

1 (1 oz.) package ranch dip mix
1 (16 oz.) container of sour cream
5 slices bacon, crisply cooked and crumbled
1 cup shredded Cheddar cheese

Combine dip package with sour cream. Stir in bacon and cheese. Refrigerate. Serve with chips.

Yield: 4 servings.

Bacon Wrapped Olives

36 large pimento-stuffed olives
18 strips bacon, thin-sliced

Cut each strip of bacon in half crosswise. Wrap an olive in bacon starting at cut end. Put wooden pick in olive to hold bacon securely. Be sure to wrap the bacon around olive so the pimento is visible. Place on pan that allows grease to drip to bottom of pan. Broil for 5 to 8 minutes or until bacon is cooked. Leave sufficient room between pan and broiler for splattering grease.

Mushroom Appetizers

1 lb. mushrooms
1 lb. cream cheese, softened
1 lb. bacon, cooked crisp and crumbled

Remove mushroom stems and chop. Combine stems, cream cheese and bacon; mix well. Fill mushroom caps with combined ingredients. Bake in preheated oven at 350 degrees F for approximately 10 minutes, then place under broiler until brown.

Yield: 15 servings.

Spinach-Bacon Spread

8 slices bacon, crisply cooked and crumbled
2 (10 oz.) packages frozen chopped spinach, thawed and well drained
4 (8 oz.) packages Monterey Jack cheese with jalapeno peppers, shredded
1 (10.75 oz.) can Cheddar cheese soup, undiluted
1 (8 oz.) package cream cheese, softened
1 teaspoon Greek seasoning
1/2 teaspoon onion powder
1 teaspoon hot sauce
1 (2 oz.) jar diced pimiento, drained
Paprika (optional)

In a bowl, combine bacon, spinach, Monterey Jack cheese, soup, cream cheese, Greek seasoning, onion powder and hot sauce. Pour in a lightly greased 11x7x2 inch baking dish; microwave at HIGH 3 minutes. Reduce heat to MEDIUM (50% power), and microwave 7 to 9 minutes, stirring at 1 1/2 minute intervals. Sprinkle mixture with pimiento and paprika, if desired. Serve spread with crackers or bagel chips.

Yield 1 1/2 quarts.

Crab Meat Bacon Rounds

2 egg whites
1/2 cup Cheddar cheese, shredded
1 (6.5 oz.) can crab meat, flaked
20 toast rounds (2"), buttered
3 strips bacon, finely diced
Stuffed green olives, sliced, for garnish

Beat egg whites until stiffly beaten. Add shredded cheese and crab meat to egg whites; mix well. Stack crab meat mixture on toast rounds. Sprinkle diced bacon on top; broil until bacon is crisp and cheese starts to melt. Top each with an olive slice.

Yield: 20 rounds.

Cheesy Bacon Dip

1 cup sour cream
1 (8 oz.) package cream cheese, softened
1 green bell pepper, chopped
3 medium tomatoes, chopped
4 green onions, thinly sliced
1 (10 oz.) jar taco sauce
2 cups shredded Cheddar cheese
1 lb. sliced bacon, crisply cooked and crumbled
Tortilla chips

In a large mixing bowl, beat sour cream and cream cheese. Spread in an ungreased 13x9x2" dish or on a 12" plate. Combine bell pepper, tomatoes, and onions. Sprinkle over the sour cream layer. Pour taco sauce over all. Top with Cheddar cheese; refrigerate. Before serving, sprinkle with bacon. Serve with tortilla chips.

Yield: 10 to 12 servings.

Apricot-Bacon Appetizers

12 slices bacon, halved horizontally
24 dried apricots
3/4 cup soy sauce
1/4 cup brown sugar, packed

Partially cook bacon. Wrap one-half slice around single, once-folded apricot. Secure with toothpick. Place on baking sheet. Bake in preheated oven at 350 degrees F, turning once, about 20 minutes or until brown and crisp. Drain on paper towel and serve immediately with combined soy sauce and brown sugar for dipping.

Yield: 24 servings.

Breakfast

Bacon Potato Bomb

1 lb. bacon
1 onion, chopped
6 potatoes, boiled and diced
6 to 8 eggs

Cook bacon in a skillet; push to one side when crisp. Brown onion until limp, push aside. Add potatoes and stir until browned. Remove bacon and crumble or cut into pieces. Crack eggs over the whole mixture and stir until done.

Yield: 6 servings.

Eggs and Bacon Casserole

1-1/2 lb. sliced bacon, cut into pieces
1/2 cup onion, chopped
3 eggs
1 1/4 cups milk
1/2 cup Bisquick
1/2 teaspoon salt
1/8 teaspoon pepper
1/2 cup Cheddar cheese, shredded

Combine all ingredients and place in greased 1 1/2-quart casserole dish. Bake in preheated oven at 375 degrees F for 30 minutes. Let stand for 5 minutes.

Yield: 4 servings.

Egg Continental

1/2 cup or more fresh bread cubes
4 to 6 hardboiled eggs
3 to 6 slices bacon
1 cup sour cream
2 tablespoons parsley, minced
1/4 teaspoon salt (optional)
1/2 to 3/4 cups grated sharp Cheddar cheese
1 (10.5 oz.) can cream of mushroom soup
1 (4 oz.) can mushrooms
1/8 teaspoon Worcestershire sauce

Cover the bottom of an 9x13x2-inch casserole dish with bread cubes. Combine remaining ingredients and pour over bread. Bake in preheated oven at 350 degrees, uncovered, for 20 to 30 minutes. This can be prepared the night before and cooked in the morning.

Yield: 4 servings.

Breakfast Pie

8 slices crisp bacon (reserve 1 tablespoon drippings)
1/2 cup cornflake crumbs
5 eggs
2 1/2 cups frozen hash browns
1/2 cup cottage cheese
1 1/2 cups shredded Swiss cheese
1/3 cup milk
1 onion, diced
1 teaspoon salt
1 teaspoon pepper

Crumble bacon and set aside. Combine crushed cornflakes with 1 tablespoon bacon drippings; set aside. In a large bowl, beat eggs until foamy. Stir in hash browns, cottage cheese, Swiss cheese, milk, onion, salt and pepper. Pour into greased 9" pie pan. Sprinkle with bacon and crumbs. Refrigerate overnight, covered. Bake, uncovered, in preheated oven at 325 degrees F for 50 minutes, until knife inserted near center comes out clean.

Yield: 6 servings.

Bacon Brunch Squares

10 slices bacon, crisply cooked and crumbled
1 can crescent rolls
3 to 4 slices Swiss cheese
3 eggs, slightly beaten
3/4 cup milk
1 to 2 tablespoons diced onion
1 teaspoon parsley flakes

Unroll the crescent roll dough and press onto the bottom and about 1/2-inch up the sides of a 7x11-inch baking pan. Lay the cheese slices on top of the dough. Combine bacon, eggs, milk, onion and parsley flakes and pour over the cheese. Bake in preheated oven at 350 degrees F for 30 minutes, or until egg mixture is set and slightly browned.

Yield: 6 servings.

Breakfast Bread

3 packages refrigerated biscuits
1 green or red bell pepper, chopped
1 onion, chopped
1 lb. bacon, cooked and crumbled
2 cups grated Mozzarella cheese
1/4 cups butter, melted

Cut biscuits in thirds. Layer biscuit pieces on the bottom of a Bundt pan; add 1/2 each of the peppers, onion, bacon and cheese. Repeat layers. Pour melted butter over top. Bake in preheated oven at 350 degrees F for 30 to 40 minutes.

Yield: 10 servings.

Baked Omelet

6 slices thin-sliced Cheddar cheese, cut in halves
8 eggs, well beaten
1 cup milk
12 slices bacon, cooked crisp (divided)
1/2 cup green bell pepper, chopped (optional)

Arrange cheese in bottom of pie pan sprayed with non-stick cooking spray. Beat eggs and milk together. Crumble 4 slices of bacon; add to egg mixture. Stir in bell pepper and pour egg mixture over cheese. Bake in preheated oven at 350 degrees F for 30 minutes. Arrange remaining bacon slices on top of omelet. Bake 10 more minutes. Let stand 5 minutes before cutting.

Yield: 4 to 6 servings.

Eggs Baked in Bacon Rings

6 slices of bacon
6 eggs
6 tablespoons chili sauce
2 tablespoons margarine or butter

In a small skillet, sauté bacon lightly. Spray muffin cups with non-stick cooking spray. Put one strip of bacon around side of each muffin cup. In the bottom of each cup, place 1 tablespoon chili sauce. Add an egg to each muffin cup and 1 teaspoon of margarine or butter. Bake in preheated oven for 15 to 20 minutes at 325 degrees F, or until egg is set. Serve on English muffins. This can be prepared the night before and baked the next day.

Yield: 6 servings.

Breakfast on A Stick

4 oz. any kind of dried fruit
1/2 cup sugar
2 teaspoons ground cinnamon
4 brown and serve rolls, unbaked and quartered
1/3 cup butter, melted
1 lb. Canadian bacon, thinly sliced
1 (16 oz.) jar spiced crab apples, drained
4 skewers

Cover dried fruit with water and let stand for 10 minutes. Drain. In a small bowl, combine sugar and cinnamon. Dip quartered brown and serve rolls into melted butter and roll in cinnamon and sugar mixture.

Starting with Canadian bacon, fold each slice into quarters and thread onto skewer. Continue threading bacon alternately with dried fruit and spiced apples. Hold and turn skewers over low coals on grill or over campfire, avoiding flame, for 10 to 12 minutes or until heated through.

Yield: 4 servings.

Breakfast Burritos

4 slices turkey bacon
2 flour tortillas (7 inches in diameter)
2 tablespoons Cheddar cheese, shredded
2 egg whites
1 tablespoon chopped mild chilies
Salsa or taco sauce (optional)
Additional shredded sharp Cheddar cheese (optional)

Over medium-high heat, cook bacon in a non-stick skillet for 8 or 9 minutes or until lightly browned. On each tortilla, place 2 turkey bacon slices, then sprinkle each with 1 tablespoon of cheese. Beat chilies with egg whites; add to hot skillet. Cook and stir for 2 minutes or until set. Split egg mixture between flour tortillas. Fold tortillas over filling. Top with additional cheese and salsa, if desired.

Yield: 2 burritos.

To keep burritos warm: Wrap filled burritos in foil and place in warm oven up to 30 minutes.

Dilly Breakfast

1 onion, chopped
2 tablespoons margarine
1 (1-lb.) loaf frozen bread dough, thawed
3 tablespoons spicy brown mustard
4 oz. Swiss cheese, shredded
6 slices bacon, crisply cooked and crumbled
1 tablespoon dill weed
2 tablespoons dill seeds
1 egg, beaten

In a skillet, brown onion in margarine. Roll the bread dough into an 8x12-inch rectangle and spread with mustard. Layer the Swiss cheese, browned onion, bacon, dill weed and half the dill seeds over the mustard.

Roll as for a jelly roll, sealing the edge. Place seam side down in a 9-inch round cake pan. Make several 1/4-inch diagonal slashes in the top of the bread. Let rise, covered, in a warm place until doubled in bulk. Brush with the beaten egg and sprinkle with remaining 1 tablespoon dill seeds. Bake in preheated oven at 375 degrees F for 25 to 30 minutes or until the bread tests done.

Yield: 12 servings.

Open-Faced Breakfast Sandwiches

1/2 cup processed cream cheese spread
4 whole wheat English muffins, split and toasted
1/2 cup orange marmalade
8 slices Canadian bacon
1 cup alfalfa sprouts
32 mandarin orange segments

Spread 1 tablespoon cream cheese on cut side of each muffin half; spread 1 tablespoon orange marmalade over cream cheese. Top with Canadian bacon; place on a baking sheet. With electric oven door partially open, broil 5" from heat for 3 minutes or until hot. Remove from oven; top each with 2 tablespoons alfalfa sprouts and 4 orange segments.

Yield: 8 servings.

Bread and Rolls

Poppy Seed Bacon Bread

1 loaf French bread
1/2 cup butter or margarine
1 medium onion, minced
4 to 5 oz. mushrooms, minced
2 tablespoons poppy seeds
1/4 cup spicy brown mustard
3/4 lb. Swiss cheese, sliced
8 slices bacon, uncooked

Trim the crust from the top and sides of the loaf. Slice the loaf lengthwise to make 2 pieces. Cut each piece at 1/2 inch intervals almost to the bottom, but not completely through. Melt the butter in a medium skillet and sauté the onions for 5 minutes over medium heat. Add the mushrooms and sauté 2 minutes more. Add the poppy seeds and mustard and stir to blend well.

Cut the cheese slices to fit the bread. Spread a heaping teaspoonful of the onion-mushroom mixture between the cuts in the bread. Place a cheese slice between the cuts in the bread. Lay the bacon on top of the bread in a criss-cross manner, and place on a baking sheet. Bake in a preheated oven at 350 degrees F for 30 minutes, or until the bacon is crisp and the cheese is melted. Yield: 2 loaves.

Bacon Braid

6 slices bacon, diced
1 package hot roll mix
1 1/2 teaspoons instant minced onion
1 (3 oz.) package cream cheese, softened
1 teaspoon milk
1 egg, beaten

Cook bacon and remove from pan when cooked but not crisp. Drain on paper towels. Following instructions on package, prepare hot roll mix, adding onion along with flour mixture. Cover and let rise in warm place until doubled in size, 30 to 45 minutes.

In a small bowl, blend cream cheese and milk until smooth. Set aside. Roll out dough on floured surface to a 12 inch square. Spread cream cheese mixture on dough and sprinkle with bacon pieces. Fold dough in half. Roll out again to a 12 inch square. Cut dough into three 4 inch strips. Pinch one end of each of the 3 strips together and braid the dough. Pinch remaining ends together.

Adjust dough to fit into a generously greased 9x5" loaf pan. Let dough rise until doubled in size, about 45 minutes. Brush beaten egg over top of loaf. Bake in preheated oven at 350 degrees F for 35 to 40 minutes or until loaf is golden brown and sounds hollow when tapped on top. Cool in pan 10 minutes before removing.

Yield: 4 servings.

Baltic Bacon Crescents

1 lb. bacon, diced
1 cup onion, chopped
1/2 teaspoon cracked black pepper
1 lb. frozen bread dough, thawed
1 egg, beaten, optional
Poppy seed, optional
Softened butter, optional

Sauté bacon and onion 2 to 3 minutes or until onion is soft but not browned. Drain well. Transfer to bowl. Add pepper and mix well. Slice dough into 8 equal pieces, then slice each into thirds. Mold each piece into a 3-inch round. Mound 1 tablespoon bacon mixture along center. Fold in half. Pinch edges together. Form into crescent shape.

Place on lightly greased baking sheets. Bake in preheated oven at 350 degrees F for 15 minutes or until lightly browned. Serve warm. If desired, glaze with beaten egg and sprinkle with poppy seeds before baking. Or, glaze top lightly with softened butter after baking.

Yield: 24 servings.

Bacon Wands

12 slices bacon
12 very thin breadsticks

Wrap bacon around the breadsticks spiral fashion. With ends of bacon down, place on a rack on a broiler pan. Bake in preheated oven at 400 degrees F for 10 minutes, or until bacon is crisp-cooked. Serve warm.

Yield: 12 sticks.

Bacon Cornettes

10 to 12 slices bacon, diced
1 cup yellow corn meal
1 cup all-purpose flour
1/4 cup sugar
4 teaspoons baking powder
3/4 teaspoon salt
2 eggs
1 cup milk
1/4 cup vegetable oil or margarine, softened

Cook bacon until crisp; drain. Combine corn meal, flour, sugar, baking powder and salt. Add eggs, milk and oil or margarine. With rotary or electric beater, beat until just smooth, about 1 minute. Add bacon and stir just until combined.

Spray muffin cups with non-stick cooking spray. Pour batter into muffin cups, filling each 2/3 full. Bake in preheated oven at 425 degrees F for 20 to 25 minutes.

Yield: 1 dozen.

Bacon Butter

1/2 cup butter
3/4 teaspoon prepared mustard
4 slices bacon, cooked crisp and crumbled

Cream the butter until light and fluffy. Blend in mustard and bacon; stir until well combined.

Yield: 1/2 cup spread.

Bacon Bars

1/2 cup shredded sharp process American cheese
6 slices bacon
2 cups packaged biscuit mix
3 tablespoons bacon drippings

In a skillet, cook bacon over medium heat until crisp and brown. Remove from skillet, drain on paper towels. Crumble bacon. Reserve bacon drippings.

Stir cheese and bacon into dry biscuit mix. Make dough according to package directions for rich biscuits, substituting bacon drippings for vegetable oil. Knead as directed for rolled biscuits. Roll to 10x6 inches. Cut in six 10-inch strips, 1-inch wide; cut each in thirds crosswise, to make 18 bars. Place 1 inch apart on ungreased baking sheet. Bake in preheated oven at 450 degrees F for 10 minutes.

Yield: 18 servings.

Broiled Olive Snacks

1 package refrigerated biscuits
3 tablespoons butter or margarine, melted
1 cup shredded sharp process American cheese
1/2 cup stuffed green olives, chopped
2 stiff-beaten egg whites
3 or 4 slices bacon, finely diced

Bake biscuits as directed on package. Split. Brush cut side with butter. Fold cheese and olives into egg whites; spoon on buttered side of biscuits. Sprinkle with bacon. Top each with an olive slice. Broil 4 to 5 inches from heat 5 to 8 minutes or until bacon browns and cheese melts.

Yield: 5 servings.

Bacon-Cheese French Bread

1 (16 oz.) loaf unsliced French bread
5 slices bacon, cooked and crumbled
2 cups shredded mozzarella cheese
1/4 cup butter or margarine, melted

Cut bread into 1 inch slices. Place sliced loaf on a large piece of aluminum foil. Combine bacon and cheese; place between bread slices. Drizzle butter over loaf, and wrap in foil. Bake in preheated oven at 350 degrees F for 20 minutes or until thoroughly heated.

Yield: 1 loaf.

Bacon Crescent Roll-Ups

1 package refrigerated crescent rolls
1/4 teaspoon onion salt
8 slices bacon, crisply cooked and crumbled

Remove rolls from package and separate. Season each with a little onion salt. Sprinkle bacon on each triangle of dough. Roll up dough, starting with wide end. Place on ungreased baking sheet with point side down. Bake in preheated oven at 375 degrees F for 12 to 15 minutes.

Yield: 8 rolls.

Main Dishes - Beef

Braciole (Italian Steak Rolls)

2 eggs
2 cups fine bread crumbs
1/2 cup shredded cheese (Parmesan or Romano)
6 slices bacon, chopped
3/4 cup celery leaves, chopped
1 teaspoon sweet basil
1/2 teaspoon salt
1/2 teaspoon garlic powder
1/2 teaspoon black pepper
1 egg, hard boiled and finely chopped
2 cups tomato juice
1 1/2 lb. round steak, sliced thin
1 (15 oz.) jar spaghetti sauce

Combine all ingredients, except steak and spaghetti sauce. Lay steak out flat and cover with filling. Roll as you would for a jellyroll, securing with toothpicks. Brown well in a skillet over medium-high heat. Pour spaghetti sauce over steak rolls; cover tightly and cook until steak is very tender, at least 1 1/2 hours. Serve with any type spaghetti or macaroni noodles. Yield: 4 servings.

Lasagna Pie

1 lb. ground beef
1/2 cup onion, chopped
1/4 cup green bell pepper, chopped
1 (15 oz.) jar spaghetti sauce
8 oz. hot, cooked macaroni or spaghetti (or any pasta)
1/3 cup grated Parmesan cheese
2 eggs, beaten
2 teaspoons butter
1 cup cottage cheese
1 (8 oz.) package Canadian bacon
1/2 cup shredded Mozzarella cheese

Brown the ground beef with the onion and bell pepper in a large skillet, stirring until the ground beef is browned; drain. Stir in the spaghetti sauce. In a large bowl, combine the pasta, Parmesan cheese, eggs and butter; mix well.

Pour the pasta mixture in a 9x13x2 inch baking pan. Spread the cottage cheese over the macaroni layer; spoon the ground beef mixture over the cottage cheese. Lay Canadian bacon over the ground beef, then sprinkle the Mozzarella cheese over the top. Bake in preheated oven at 350 degrees F for 20 minutes, or until the cheese melts.

Yield: 4 servings.

Quick Stroganoff

4 slices bacon, diced
1 1/2 lb. ground beef
1 large onion
1 cup cream of mushroom soup
3/4 teaspoon salt
1/4 teaspoon paprika
1 1/2 tablespoons flour
1/8 teaspoon pepper
1/2 pint sour cream
Egg noodles

Brown bacon and ground beef, then add onion. Spoon off fat and add mushroom soup. Add salt, paprika, flour and pepper and stir. Simmer uncovered for 20 minutes, stirring often. Stir in sour cream and heat for 5 minutes or until hot. Serve over noodles or toast.

Yield: 6 servings.

Bacon-Wrapped Little Loaves

1 1/2 lbs. ground beef
1 egg
1 cup shredded Cheddar cheese
1/2 cup water
1/4 cup onion, chopped
1/4 cup lemon juice
1/4 cup green bell pepper, chopped
1/4 cup dry bread crumbs
1 teaspoon salt
1/2 teaspoon instant beef bouillon
6 slices bacon, thinly-sliced

Combine all ingredients except bacon. Form into six loaves. Cross two half-slices of bacon on each little loaf, tucking the bacon ends under loaf. Place loaves on a rack in a baking pan. Bake in preheated oven at 350 degrees F uncovered for 50 minutes.

Yield: 6 servings.

Stuffed Peppers

6 or 7 large peppers
1/2 lb. bacon, diced
1 1/2 lb. ground beef
1 onion, diced
Tops from peppers, diced
Salt and pepper
1/2 teaspoon oregano
1 teaspoon chili powder
1/4 teaspoon minced garlic
1/2 teaspoon sweet basil
3 cups cooked rice
Tomato sauce or chili sauce
1/2 lb. sharp processed cheese, shredded

In a large skillet, cook diced bacon. Cut the tops off peppers and dice the tops. Add ground beef, onion, pepper tops and spices and sauté until done. Add rice, tomato or chili sauce, and cheese. Mix well.

Parboil peppers in boiling water for 3 to 5 minutes. Spoon mixture into parboiled peppers. Sprinkle with grated Parmesan cheese. Bake in preheated oven for 20 to 30 minutes at 350 degrees.

Yield: 4 to 6 servings.

Meat Sauce for Spaghetti

6 slices bacon, diced
1 lb. ground beef
1/4 cup onion, chopped
1/2 cup celery, chopped
2 cloves garlic, finely chopped
3 to 4 cups tomatoes
1 (8 oz.) can tomato sauce
2 teaspoons salt
1/4 teaspoon black pepper
1/2 teaspoon paprika
Small piece bay leaf
1/8 teaspoon cayenne pepper (optional)

Brown bacon, beef, onion, celery and garlic, stirring frequently. Add tomatoes, tomato sauce, salt, black pepper, paprika, bay leaf and cayenne pepper. Simmer about 1 1/2 hours. Add a few drops of Tabasco if hotter sauce is desired.

Yield: 4 servings.

Liver and Onions

1 lb. beef liver
1/4 cup flour
1 teaspoon salt
1/8 teaspoon pepper
6 slices bacon
1 cup onion, chopped

Combine flour, salt, and pepper. Coat liver with flour mixture. Place bacon and onion in a 10-inch microwavable dish. Cook in microwave oven, covered, for 8 to 10 minutes, or until bacon is almost crisp. Remove bacon and onion. Add liver to bacon drippings. Cook in microwave oven for 8 minutes. Turn liver over halfway through cooking time. Put onion and bacon on top of liver. Cook in microwave oven for 1 minute, or until heated through.

Yield: 4 servings.

Cavatini

4 small packages pasta shapes
1 lb. sausage (mild or Italian)
1 lb. ground beef
1 package Canadian bacon slices
1 package small pepperoni slices
2 (4 oz.) cans mushroom slices
1 small onion, diced
1 small bell pepper, diced
2 (26 oz. each) jars chunky spaghetti sauce
6 cups Mozzarella cheese

Boil pasta according to directions; drain and put in large bowl. Brown sausage and ground beef; drain. Combine with pasta, Canadian bacon, pepperoni, mushrooms, onions, and bell pepper. Mix all ingredients thoroughly; stir in spaghetti sauce.

Place in 9x13x2 inch pan; top with cheese and bake in preheated oven at 350 degrees F until cheese melts. Or put in crockpot, layering cheese and mixture, on low setting. If it gets a little dried out, may add tomato juice or more spaghetti sauce. Makes a huge batch and is perfect for large dinners, potlucks, and also freezes well.

Yield: 8 to 12 servings.

Snow-Capped Franks

2 cups mashed potatoes
2 tablespoons onion, grated
2 tablespoons parsley, chopped
1 teaspoon prepared mustard
1 package of 10 hot dogs
4 slices bacon, crisply cooked and crumbled

Use leftover potatoes or prepare instant mashed potatoes as directed on package. Mix potatoes, onion, parsley and mustard. Cut hot dogs lengthwise, being careful not to cut completely through. Flatten franks completely and spread with potato mixture. Garnish with crumbled bacon. Broil about 8 minutes, until tips of potatoes are browned.

Yield: 4 servings.

Beans and Burger Bake

2 slices bacon, diced
1/4 cup onion, chopped
1 lb. ground beef
2 (16 oz.) cans beans in molasses sauce
1/4 teaspoon salt
1/2 cup molasses
1/2 cup ketchup
1/2 teaspoon dry mustard
1/8 teaspoon Worcestershire sauce

Sauté bacon over medium-high heat until cooked crisp. Remove bacon and sauté onions and ground beef in bacon drippings. Drain off excess fat and juices. Combine bacon, onion and beef with remaining ingredients in 1 1/2-quart casserole. Bake uncovered in preheated oven at 350 degrees F for 45 minutes.

Yield: 6 to 8 servings.

Buffet Beef Rolls

1 egg, beaten
1 teaspoon seasoned salt
1 teaspoon onion salt
1/8 teaspoon pepper
2 lbs. ground beef
8 slices (4" squares) Swiss cheese
8 thin slices Canadian bacon
1 egg
1 cup herb seasoned bread crumbs
Vegetable oil
1 (10.75 oz.) can golden mushroom soup
1/2 cup dry red wine

Stir together egg, seasoned salt, onion salt and pepper. Add meat and mix well. Shape into eight 4" square patties, 1/4" thick. Press 1 cheese slice on top, then 1 bacon slice. Roll jelly roll fashion, seal seam and ends. Beat remaining egg with 2 tablespoons water. Dip rolls in egg, then in crumbs. Brown rolls in hot oil then place in 9 x 13 baking dish.

Discard oil in skillet - heat soup and wine. Pour over rolls, cover, refrigerate overnight. Bake in preheated oven uncovered, at 350 degrees F for 1 1/4 hours, baste occasionally.

Yield: 8 servings.

5-Deck Dinner

6 slices of bacon
3/4 lb. ground beef
1/8 teaspoon salt
1/8 teaspoon pepper
4 medium onions, sliced
4 medium potatoes, sliced
4 to 6 carrots, sliced or 1 cup canned corn
1/4 cup green bell pepper, chopped
1/4 tablespoon parsley, chopped
1/4 cup water
1 (15 oz.) can tomato sauce (optional)

Cut bacon into 1" pieces; line bacon in bottom of heavy skillet or Dutch oven. Make ground beef into patties and lay on top of bacon; season with salt and pepper. Add layers of onions, potatoes and carrots or corn.

Season each layer with salt and pepper. Scatter bell pepper and chopped parsley over top. Place skillet on medium heat and cook 3 minutes after bacon begins to sizzle. Add 1/4 cup water (and optional tomato sauce). Cover and turn heat on low. Cook for 30 to 40 minutes on low.

Yield: 4 servings.

Main Dishes - Seafood

Iowa Baked Catfish

6 pan-dressed catfish fillets
3 slices bacon, crisply cooked and crumbled
1/2 cup onion, minced
1/4 cup green bell pepper, minced
1/2 teaspoon salt
1/8 teaspoon pepper
1 1/2 cups fresh bread crumbs
1 (8 oz.) can cream style corn
1 (8 oz.) can whole corn, drained
1 egg, beaten
3 slices bacon, cut in half, uncooked

Place fish in a greased 15x10" baking pan. Cook bacon and reserve 2 tablespoons drippings. Add onion and bell pepper to bacon drippings. Cook until tender. Stir in salt, pepper, bread crumbs, corn, egg and bacon. Put this stuffing into fish cavity. Place 1/2 slice bacon on top of each fish. Bake in preheated oven at 400 degrees F for 25 minutes or until fish flakes easily.

Yield: 4 to 6 servings.

Shrimp and Grits

2 cups milk
1/2 cup quick-cooking 5-minute grits
4 oz. Monterey Jack cheese, grated
4 tablespoons butter
6 strips bacon
1 tablespoon vegetable oil
1/2 onion, diced
4 cloves garlic, minced
1 lb. shrimp, peeled and deveined (31 to 35 medium or large)
Salt and pepper, to taste
Tabasco sauce, to taste

Bring milk to a boil in a saucepan. Slowly add the grits while stirring. When all the grits have been added, reduce the heat to low. Lay the cheese on top, cover, and simmer for 5 minutes. Add the butter; salt and pepper to taste. Stir well.

In a large skillet, cook bacon over medium-high heat. Remove bacon and transfer to paper towels (leave bacon drippings in skillet). Crumble bacon when cool. Add vegetable oil, onion and garlic and cook for 2 to 3 minutes, or until onions are translucent. Add shrimp and cook, stirring frequently, for approximately 4 minutes (shrimp will turn pink when cooked). Season with salt, pepper and Tabasco sauce. To serve, spoon grits onto plates; top with shrimp mixture. Sprinkle crumbled bacon over shrimp.

Yield: 4 servings.

Main Dishes - Pork

Tenderloin Supreme

12 slices bacon
6 pork tenderloin patties, 1" thick
6 slices tomato, cut 1/2" thick
6 slices onion, cut 1/4" thick
Salt and pepper, to taste

Prepare each serving as follows: Cross two slices of bacon at right angles. Place pork patty in the center of the bacon; season with salt and pepper. Place a slice of tomato on the patty and season; top with a slice of onion. Bring the ends of the bacon up over the top and fasten with a wooden toothpick.

Place patties in a baking dish, cover with foil, and bake in preheated oven at 350 degrees F for 30 minutes. Remove foil and continue baking for 30 to 45 minutes longer.

Yield: 4 to 6 servings.

Chuckalaya

1/2 lb. bacon cut in pieces
1 medium onion, diced
8 oz. fresh mushrooms, sliced
1/2 green bell pepper, diced
2 tablespoons olive oil
1 heaping tablespoon flour
1 (14 oz.) can diced tomatoes
1 cup water
3 cups cooked rice
3 cups smoked ham, chopped
2 cups chorizo sausage (sliced in quarter size)
2 cups peeled shrimp
Creole seasoning
Cayenne pepper
Worcestershire sauce

In a large skillet, sauté bacon and onion. Cook at low temperature until brown. Add mushrooms, pepper and olive oil. Let peppers and mushrooms cook down. Stir in flour and add tomatoes and water. Stir until the mixture thickens somewhat. Then stir in rice, ham and sausage. Cover and continue to simmer about 15 minutes. Add the shrimp. Season to taste with creole seasoning, cayenne pepper and Worcestershire sauce. Simmer over low heat. If it seems too dry, more water may be added.

Yield: 6 servings.

Poor Man's Stew

1/2 lb. bacon
1 large onion
2 or 3 large potatoes, sliced
1 small head of cabbage, cut-up or wedge

Combine all ingredients together in a heavy pan with lid. Steam for an hour or until vegetables are tender.

Yield: 2 servings.

Dublin Coddle

1/2 lb. bacon
1 lb. smoked sausages
1/2 cup all-purpose flour
2 teaspoons dried parsley (divided)
1/2 teaspoon salt
1/2 teaspoon pepper
4 medium potatoes, peeled and cut into thick slices
2 medium carrots, peeled and cut into thick slices
1 clove garlic, minced
1 cup beef broth

Cut bacon slices into quarters; cook in skillet until soft and partially cooked. Remove bacon and place in stockpot. Slice sausages into large pieces. Combine flour, 1 teaspoon parsley, salt and pepper. Dip pieces of sausage into flour mixture. Fry in bacon drippings. Add sausage to stockpot. Add potatoes, carrots, garlic, 1 teaspoon parsley, and broth. With a large spoon, gently mix meats and vegetables. Cover and simmer on top of stove for 60 minutes.

Yield: 6 servings.

Hearty Hodgepodge

6 slices bacon
1 medium onion, thinly sliced
1 lb. beef shank
3/4 lb. ham hock
6 cups water
2 teaspoons salt
2 (15 oz. each) cans garbanzo beans
3 cups potatoes, diced
1 clove garlic, minced
1 (4 oz.) link Polish sausage, thinly sliced

Cook bacon until crisp and set aside. Reserve 2 tablespoons drippings. Crumble bacon. Add sliced onion to drippings in pan. Cook until tender but not brown; add beef and ham, water and salt. Cover and simmer 1 1/2 hours. Remove meat from bone. Skim off fat. Add undrained beans, potatoes and garlic. Simmer 30 minutes. Add sausage and bacon. Simmer 15 minutes. Serve with toasted and buttered French bread.

Yield: 10 servings.

Jambalaya

4 slices bacon
6 link sausages
1 large onion, coarsely chopped
1 large clove garlic, minced
1 stalk celery, finely diced
1 green bell pepper, diced
1 cup uncooked rice
2 tablespoons tomato paste
1 (14.5 oz.) can chicken broth
1 (14.5 oz.) can Italian style tomatoes
1/2 teaspoon thyme
1/2 teaspoon salt
1/8 teaspoon ground cloves
1/4 teaspoon pepper
1/4 teaspoon chili powder
4 to 6 drops Tabasco
2 cups ham, diced
1/4 cup parsley, minced

Cut bacon into 1 inch pieces. Cut sausages into 1/2-inch slices. Sauté together in a large skillet or stockpot until brown. Remove meat. Pour off all but 2 tablespoons drippings. Add onion, garlic, celery and bell pepper. Sauté until onion is soft. Add rice. Stir until well mixed. Add tomato paste, chicken broth, tomatoes with juice, thyme, salt, cloves, pepper, chili powder and Tabasco. Bring to a boil.

Add ham, sausages, bacon and parsley. Pour into a 2 quart baking dish. Cover tightly. Bake at 350 degrees F for approximately 1 hour. Check from time to time to make sure there is enough liquid. Add 1/4 cup water if necessary. Serve when liquid has been absorbed and rice is tender.

Yield: 6 servings.

Variation:

Substitute 2 cups cooked chicken or shrimp. Stir into skillet only about 10 minutes before removing from oven in order not to overcook.

Main Dishes - Chicken

Louisiana Chicken

4 slices bacon
1 small green bell pepper, sliced
1/2 cup onion, chopped
1 (10.75 oz.) can tomato soup
1/2 cup water
1 1/2 cups chicken, diced and cooked

In a large skillet, cook bacon until crisp; drain on paper towels, then crumble. Cook bell pepper and onion in bacon drippings until tender. Stir in tomato soup, water, chicken and half the bacon pieces. Cook, stirring occasionally, over medium-high heat until chicken is cooked and juices run clear. Serve over cooked rice. Garnish with remaining bacon.

Yield: About 3 cups.

Party Chicken

4 chicken breasts, boneless and skinless
8 slices ham
8 slices American cheese
8 slices bacon
1 cup sour cream
1 cup cream of mushroom soup

Cut each chicken breast in half and pound each until flattened. Top each chicken breast with 1 slice of ham and American cheese. Roll up and wrap a slice of bacon around each breast and secure with a toothpick. Place in a greased baking dish. Combine sour cream and soup and pour over the top of the chicken. Bake covered one hour and one more hour uncovered at 325 degrees.

Yield: 8 servings.

Rizotto Corine – Rice with Chicken and Vegetables

6 bacon slices, diced
1/4 cup butter
2 chicken breasts, boneless and skinless, cut into strips
2 medium onions, cut into thin rings
2 large green bell peppers, chopped
1 (8 oz.) can mushroom pieces
1 2/3 cups long grain rice, soaked in cold water for 30 minutes and drained
1 (15 oz.) can of tomatoes with liquid
1 (10 oz.) can sweet corn, drained
1 teaspoon salt
1/2 teaspoon black pepper
1/2 teaspoon thyme
1/4 teaspoon celery salt
1/4 teaspoon cayenne pepper
2 teaspoons Worcestershire sauce (optional)
1 (15 oz.) can chicken stock
1/4 cup Parmesan cheese, grated

In a large skillet, cook bacon over moderate heat for 5 minutes. Drain on paper towels; set aside. Add half the butter to the bacon drippings in skillet; add chicken strips. Stir fry for 6 to 8 minutes or until lightly browned. Remove and set aside. Next, stir fry onions and peppers for 5 minutes. Add mushrooms and stir for 3 more minutes. Remove the vegetables and set aside.

Add the remaining butter to the pan and fry the rice, stirring constantly for 3 minutes. Stir in the chicken, bacon, vegetables, tomatoes, sweet corn, salt, pepper, thyme, celery salt, cayenne pepper and Worcestershire sauce. Pour in the chicken stock. Bring to a boil, stirring constantly. Reduce heat to very low. Cover and simmer for 20 minutes or until rice is done. Serve with the Parmesan cheese.

Yield: 2 to 4 servings.

Soups and Sandwiches

Cheesy Potato Soup

1 cup carrots, sliced thin
1 cup celery, chopped
1 cup onions, chopped
1 lb. bacon, crisply cooked and crumbled
4 cups water
32 oz. frozen cubed hash browns
1 lb. processed cheese
2 cans evaporated milk
1 cup ham, cubed
1/2 cup flour
1/2 cup water
Salt and pepper to taste

Boil carrots, celery and onions for 15 minutes. Drain. Set aside.

Combine water, bacon, veggies and hash browns in a large pot. Bring to a boil; reduce heat and simmer. Add cheese, milk and ham. Simmer. Mix 1/2 cup flour in water and add to soup to thicken. Add salt and pepper to taste.

Yield: 4 servings.

Bacon Vegetable Soup

1/2 lb. bacon, chopped
1/2 lb. mushrooms, sliced
1 medium onion, chopped
4 cups canned chicken broth
2 potatoes, peeled and cut into julienne strips
1 large carrot, cut into julienne strips
1 bay leaf
1/4 teaspoon ground red pepper
1/2 cup whipping cream
1 tablespoon cornstarch
1 1/2 cups lightly packed shredded romaine lettuce

In a 5 to 6-quart pan, cook bacon over medium heat until crisp; drain, reserving 2 tablespoons bacon drippings. Add mushrooms and onion to drippings in pan; cook, stirring often, until onion is soft and most of the liquid has evaporated, about 10 minutes.

Stir in chicken broth, potatoes, carrot, bay leaf and red pepper. Stir together cream and cornstarch; stir into soup. Bring to a boil over high heat, stirring constantly; reduce heat and simmer, uncovered, stirring occasionally, until carrot and potatoes are tender (about 5 minutes). Garnish individual servings with romaine lettuce.

Yield: 4 servings.

New England Clam Chowder

3 (7.5 oz.) cans minced clams
6 slices bacon
4 cups potatoes, diced
1 1/2 cups water
1/2 cup onion, chopped
1 cup light cream
2 cups milk (divided)
6 tablespoons flour
1 1/2 teaspoons salt
1/8 teaspoon pepper

Drain clams, reserving 1/2 cup of liquid. In a large saucepan, cook bacon until crisp. Remove, crumble and set aside. To drippings in pan, add reserved clam liquid, potatoes, water and onion. Cook, covered, for 20 minutes or until potatoes are tender.

Add clams, cream and 1 1/2 cups of milk. In a bowl, blend remaining 1/2 cup milk with flour; then stir into chowder. Cook until boiling; stirring occasionally. Add salt and pepper. Sprinkle with bacon.

Yield: 6 servings.

Super Corn Soup

5 slices bacon
1 medium onion, thinly sliced, separate rings
2 cups whole kernel corn (cooked)
1 cup diced cooked potatoes
1 (10.5 oz.) can cream of mushroom soup
2 1/2 cups milk
1 teaspoon salt
1/8 teaspoon pepper

Cook bacon until crisp. Remove bacon from pan; pour off drippings leaving 2 tablespoons in pan. Add onion and cook until lightly browned. Add corn, potatoes, soup, milk, salt and pepper. Heat to boiling, reduce heat and simmer a minute. Top each serving with crumbled bacon and a dot of butter.

Yield: 4 servings.

Squash and Pea Soup

1 cup dry split peas
3 slices bacon, cut up
1 cup onion, chopped
1 cup green bell pepper, chopped
1 teaspoon instant chicken bouillon granules
4 cups water
3/4 teaspoon salt
1/8 teaspoon pepper
1 (12 oz.) package frozen mashed squash
1 cup light cream

Rinse peas; set aside. In a large saucepan, cook bacon until crisp; drain, reserving drippings in pan. Set bacon aside. Cook onion and bell pepper in drippings just until tender; add peas, bouillon granules, water, salt and pepper. Bring to boiling. Reduce heat; cover and simmer for 1 1/2 hours. Stir in frozen squash; cover and simmer 20 minutes or until heated through. Stir in cream and bacon; heat through.

Yield: 4 servings.

Wild Rice Soup

1 lb. bacon
1 cup celery, diced
1 cup onion, chopped
2 (14.5 oz.) cans chicken broth
2 (10.5 oz.) cans cream of mushroom soup
1 (7 oz.) box of wild rice

Cook bacon until crisp; reserve 2 tablespoons of bacon drippings and sauté celery and onion in the drippings; set aside. In a large pan, heat chicken broth and cream of mushroom soup; add crumbled bacon, celery and onion. Cook a small box of wild rice and add to the above mixture. Fresh mushrooms may be added.

Yield: 4 servings.

Mushroom Soup

1/2 lb. bacon
1 large onion, chopped
1 lb. mushrooms, sliced
2 carrots, sliced
2 cups water
2 cups potatoes, diced
2 cups milk
Butter, salt and pepper to taste

Sauté bacon until well done. Remove bacon and some of the drippings from pan. Add onions and sauté until transparent. Remove onions from pan. In same pan, cook mushrooms, carrots and water about 20 minutes or until tender. Add potatoes and continue to cook until tender. Do not overcook. Add milk, onion and bacon. Bring to simmer and thicken to suit. Add butter, salt and pepper to taste.

Yield: 4 servings.

Beer Cheese Soup

1/3 lb. bacon, diced
1 large onion, coarsely chopped
3 quarts (12 cups) water
5 oz. extra-rich non-dairy creamer
1 tablespoon Tabasco sauce
1 tablespoon Worcestershire sauce
2 oz. chicken bouillon granules
2 (15 oz.) jars processed cheese sauce
Cornstarch to thicken
1 (12 oz.) bottle beer

Sauté bacon and onion in a skillet; drain and set aside. In a soup pot, bring water, creamer, Tabasco sauce, Worcestershire sauce and chicken bouillon to a boil. Add the sautéed bacon and onions to the pot, boil 15 minutes.

Stir in the cheese until melted. Add beer. Mix cornstarch with a little water and thicken to desired consistency, stirring constantly. Stir frequently to avoid scorching. Serve topped with popcorn, if desired.

Yield: About 1 gallon.

New England Fish Chowder

2 lb. halibut fillets
2 cups water
2 1/2 teaspoons salt
3 cups pared potatoes
6 slices bacon, chopped
1 large onion, chopped
2 cups milk
2 cups light cream
1/4 teaspoon pepper

Place fish with water in large saucepan; bring to boiling. Reduce heat; simmer, covered, 15 minutes or until fish flakes easily with fork. Remove fish, set aside.

To fish broth add 1 teaspoon salt and pared potatoes; boil, covered, about 8 minutes or until almost tender. Meanwhile, sauté bacon until crisp; drain on paper towels. Sauté onion in bacon fat until tender, about 5 minutes. Flake fish with a fork. Add fish, onion, bacon, remaining 1 1/2 teaspoons salt, milk, cream and pepper to potatoes; slowly bring to a boil. Reduce heat; simmer, uncovered for 15 minutes.

Yield: 4 servings.

Sopa De Frijol Negro
(Black Bean Soup)

1 cup dry black beans
6 cups water
4 slices bacon
1 clove garlic, minced
1/2 cup onion, chopped
1 large tomato, chopped
2 teaspoons salt
1/2 teaspoon dried oregano, crushed
1/4 teaspoon crushed red pepper
1/8 teaspoon black pepper
1/3 cup dry sherry
Lime or lemon slices

In a 3-quart saucepan, combine beans and water; soak overnight. (Or, cover and simmer 2 minutes. Remove from heat; cover and let stand 1 hour.) Do not drain. Simmer, covered, for 2 1/2 to 3 hours or until beans are tender.

In a small skillet, cook bacon over medium heat until crisp; drain, reserving 2 tablespoons bacon drippings. Cook garlic and onion in reserved drippings until tender. Add to beans along with tomato, salt, oregano, red pepper and black pepper. Cover; simmer 30 minutes.

Press bean mixture through sieve or process in blender, half at a time, until smooth. Return to saucepan; stir in sherry. Heat 5 to 10 minutes or until hot. Garnish with crumbled bacon and lime or lemon slices. Yield: 4 to 6 servings.

Corn Chowder

3 to 5 slices bacon
Small onion, chopped
1 quart milk
4 to 5 medium potatoes, diced
1 (14.75 oz.) can cream style corn
1 (15.25 oz.) can corn
Salt and pepper to taste

In a skillet over medium-high heat, cook bacon until crisp; set aside. Remove 1 or 2 pieces of bacon for garnish. Add onion to bacon drippings in skillet and cook until transparent. Add milk and potatoes and cook gently until potatoes are tender, about 20 minutes. Add corn and bacon; season to taste with salt and pepper. Garnish servings with a bit of crumbled bacon, parsley or chopped chives.

Yield: 4 servings.

Salads and Dressings

Broccoli-Raisin Salad

1 cup raisins
10 slices bacon, cooked crisp and crumbled
1 cup Miracle Whip salad dressing
2 tablespoons vinegar
1 head fresh broccoli, cut into bite-size pieces
1 small onion, chopped
1/3 cups sugar
1 cup sunflower seeds (optional)

Combine all ingredients and refrigerate.

Yield: 2 to 3 servings.

Sweet and Sour Chicken Salad

10 slices of bacon
3/4 cup granulated sugar
3/4 cup cider vinegar
1/4 teaspoon seasoned pepper
1 teaspoon celery seed
1/4 teaspoon dill seed
2 tablespoons onion, grated
1/2 cup green bell pepper, cut into 1/4 inch cubes
1/2 cup canned pimientos, cut into small pieces
2 cups chicken, cooked and diced
3 cups cooked hot fluffy rice
3 hardboiled eggs, peeled and sliced

Cook bacon in a skillet over low heat. Sauté until the bacon is very crisp; remove it from skillet. To the bacon drippings in the skillet, add sugar, vinegar and seasoned pepper. Stir and cook over low heat until the sugar is all dissolved. Add the celery seed, dill seed, onion, bell pepper and pimientos.

Continue to cook over low heat and stir in chicken. When heated through, spread the hot rice on a platter and pour the chicken mixture over it. Crumble the pieces of bacon and sprinkle on top. Arrange the egg slices around the edge of the platter.

Yield: 6 servings.

B.L.T Chicken Salad

8 cups salad greens
2 large tomatoes, chopped
2 lb. chicken breasts, boneless and skinless, cooked and cubed
12 strips bacon, cooked crisp and crumbled
4 hard-cooked eggs, sliced

In a large salad bowl, add above ingredients in layers. Dressing may be drizzled over or served in a separate bowl.

Dressing:
1 cup mayonnaise
7 tablespoons barbecue sauce
4 tablespoons onion, finely chopped
2 tablespoons lemon juice
1/4 teaspoon pepper

Mix above dressing ingredients and refrigerate.

Yield: 4 servings.

Hot German Potato Salad

6 medium potatoes, cooked and cubed
2 hard-boiled eggs, chopped
1/2 green bell pepper, chopped
1 medium onion, chopped
1 cup celery, chopped
2 tablespoons parsley
5 slices bacon
Salt and pepper, to taste

Cook bacon until crisp; crumble. (Leave bacon drippings in pan for dressing.) In a bowl, combine all ingredients above; mix well.

Dressing:
1/2 cup sugar
4 tablespoons flour
1/2 cup vinegar
1/2 cup water

Add sugar and flour to the bacon drippings. Stir well. Add vinegar and water; cook until thick. Pour over salad. Heat through.

Yield: 8 servings.

Spinach Salad with Mustard-Bacon Dressing

1 cup mayonnaise
1 small onion, finely grated
1/4 cup vegetable oil
1/4 cup red wine vinegar
3 tablespoons sugar
1 tablespoon Dijon-style mustard
Salt and pepper, to taste
1 lb. bacon, cooked crisp and crumbled
3 tablespoons bacon drippings
2 lb. spinach
1 1/2 lb. mushrooms, sliced
6 hard-boiled eggs, sliced
1/2 cup grated Parmesan cheese

Combine mayonnaise, onion, oil, vinegar, sugar, mustard, salt and pepper in small bowl; mix well. Stir in bacon drippings. Wash spinach; remove stems. Tear into bite-sized pieces. Combine with mushrooms and eggs in salad bowl. Pour mayonnaise mixture over salad; toss gently. Sprinkle with crumbled bacon and Parmesan cheese.

Yield: 12 servings.

Chili Corn Bread Salad

1 (8 oz.) package corn bread mix
1 (4 oz.) can chopped green chiles
1/8 teaspoon ground cumin
1/8 teaspoon oregano
1 (1 oz.) package ranch salad dressing mix
1 cup sour cream
1 cup mayonnaise
1 (15 oz.) can pinto beans, rinsed and drained
2 (15 oz. each) cans whole kernel corn, drained
1 cup green onions, chopped
1 cup green bell pepper, chopped
3 tomatoes, chopped
2 cups shredded Cheddar cheese
10 slices bacon, cooked crisp and crumbled

Prepare the corn bread mix using the package directions, stirring the undrained chiles, cumin and oregano into the batter before baking. Pour the batter into an 8x8-inch baking dish. Bake in preheated oven at 400 degrees F for 20 to 25 minutes. Let cool.

In a large bowl, combine salad dressing mix, sour cream and mayonnaise. Crumble half the corn bread into a 9x13x2" baking dish. Layer half the beans, sour cream mixture, corn, onions, bell pepper, tomatoes, cheese and bacon. Repeat the layers. Refrigerate, covered, for 2 hours.

Yield: 12 to 16 servings.

Bacon-Romaine Toss

1/2 lb. bacon, cooked crisp and crumbled
1 cup Swiss or Cheddar cheese, cubed
1 small red onion, chopped
2 heads romaine lettuce

Dressing:

2 tablespoons bacon drippings
2 tablespoons sugar
1 cup mayonnaise

Combine bacon, cheese, onion and lettuce in large bowl. In separate bowl, combine dressing ingredients. (May use blender for dressing.) Add dressing to lettuce and toss lightly.

Yield: 4 to 6 servings.

Baked Potato Salad

1 cup bacon, diced
8 cups potatoes, cooked and diced
1 cup onion, diced
1 cup celery, diced
3 1/2 teaspoons salt
3 tablespoons flour
1 1/3 cups water
2/3 cup vinegar
2/3 cup sugar
1/2 teaspoon pepper

In a large skillet, cook bacon, drain; return 4 tablespoons bacon drippings to pan. Cook onion and celery in bacon drippings; add salt and flour. Cook gently. Add water, vinegar, sugar, and pepper. Bring to a boil. Combine potatoes and bacon in 3-quart dish. Pour vinegar mixture over potatoes mixture. Cover and bake in preheated oven at 350 degrees F for 35 to 40 minutes.

Yield: 18 servings.

Easy Slaw

1 cup mayonnaise
4 tablespoons sugar
4 tablespoons vinegar
1 lb. cabbage
1 cup raisins
1 (3 oz.) package sunflower seeds (shelled)
6 to 8 pieces bacon, cooked and crumbled

Combine the mayonnaise, sugar and vinegar for the dressing; set aside. Stir together cabbage, raisins, sunflower seeds and bacon. Spoon half the dressing into the dry ingredients and stir well. Add the remaining dressing a few tablespoons at a time until you get the taste and consistency that you like. Refrigerate prior to serving.

Yield: 4 servings.

Mushroom-Bacon Salad

1 lb. medium-size fresh mushrooms
1/4 cup green onions, thinly sliced
2/3 cup vegetable oil or olive oil
4 tablespoons lemon juice
1 teaspoon Worcestershire sauce
1/2 teaspoon salt
1/8 teaspoon pepper
1/2 teaspoon dry mustard
1 (8 oz.) package shredded lettuce
12 slices bacon

Thinly slice mushrooms, cut from base to top. Blend rest of ingredients, except for bacon, and pour over mushrooms. Toss, cover and refrigerate at least 4 hours. Stir several times. Just before serving, cook bacon until crisp. Crumble bacon; toss with salad and lettuce.

Yield: 6 to 8 servings.

Loaded Spinach Salad

1/3 cup vegetable oil
3/4 cup sugar
1/4 cup white vinegar
1/3 cup ketchup
1 teaspoon Worcestershire sauce
1 medium onion, minced
1 bunch fresh spinach, stemmed and rinsed
2 hard-cooked eggs, diced
3/4 cup bacon, crisply cooked and crumbled
Fresh mushrooms, cleaned and sliced

Combine oil, sugar, vinegar, ketchup, Worcestershire sauce and onion in a glass jar; shake well and refrigerate. Toss spinach, eggs, bacon and mushrooms in a bowl. Pour dressing over salad and serve. Refrigerate any leftover dressing.

Yield: 4 servings.

7-Layer Salad

1/2 head lettuce, chopped
1/2 cup green bell pepper
1/2 cup onions, chopped
1/2 cup celery, chopped
1 (8.5 oz.) can peas
4 hardboiled eggs, chopped
1 (4 oz.) can water chestnuts, grated
8 to 10 slices bacon, crisply cooked and crumbled
2 tablespoons sugar
2 cups mayonnaise
4 to 6 oz. Cheddar cheese, shredded

Layer first 7 ingredients in order in a glass bowl or 9x13" baking dish. Combine sugar and mayonnaise; spread over vegetable mixture. Add crumbled bacon as the next layer. Top with cheese, cover with foil. Refrigerate for 8 to 24 hours.

Yield: 4 servings.

Hot Bacon Dressing

4 strips bacon, crisply cooked and drained
1 egg
1/2 cup sugar
1 teaspoon salt
2 tablespoons flour
1/2 cup apple cider vinegar
1 1/2 cups water
1 tablespoon prepared mustard

Combine all ingredients, except bacon, in a saucepan; cook over medium heat, stirring until thickened. Add crumbled bacon and serve over any greens – lettuce, spinach, etc.

Yield: 4 servings.

Spinach Salad

20 oz. spinach and curly lettuce
3 hard-boiled eggs
1/2 lb. bacon, cooked crisp and crumbled
1 (14 oz.) can bean sprouts, drained
1 (4 oz.) can sliced water chestnuts, drained
1 small red onion
Diced fresh mushrooms

Combine all ingredients together.

Dressing:
1 cup vegetable oil
1/4 cup wine vinegar
1/3 cup ketchup
1/2 cup sugar
1 tablespoon Worcestershire sauce
1 teaspoon salt

Mix all ingredients for dressing together well; pour over salad just before serving.

Yield: 4 servings.

Vegetables

Green Bean-Tomato Bake

1 cup cracker crumbs
1 (16 oz.) can whole tomatoes, drained with liquid reserved
3 tablespoons flour
1 (10.5 oz.) can cream of mushroom soup
1 cup sour cream
1 small onion, chopped
1 teaspoon salt
1/8 teaspoon pepper
4 slices bacon, crisply cooked and crumbled
1 (16 oz.) can whole green beans, drained
2 tablespoons butter

Sprinkle 1/2 cup cracker crumbs on bottom of buttered 1 1/2-quart casserole dish. Blend juice from tomatoes and flour. Stir in soup, sour cream, onion, salt, pepper and bacon to make a sauce. Alternate layers of green beans, tomatoes and sauce in casserole dish. Sprinkle remaining cracker crumbs on top. Bake in preheated oven at 350 degrees F for 30 minutes.

Yield: 4 servings.

Asparagus Roll-Ups

12 slices white bread, crusts trimmed
8 oz. onion-and-chive-flavored cream cheese, softened
8 slices bacon, crisply cooked and crumbled
1 (15 oz.) can long asparagus spears
1/4 cup margarine, melted
1/2 cup Parmesan cheese, grated

Flatten each slice of the bread with a rolling pin. Combine the cream cheese and bacon in a small bowl; mix well. Spread bacon mixture on the bread slices, covering to the edges. Place one large or two small asparagus spears on each bread slice.

Roll as for a jelly roll and place seam side down on a baking sheet. Brush with margarine and sprinkle with Parmesan cheese. Bake in preheated oven at 400 degrees F for 12 minutes or until lightly browned. Cut into bite-size pieces.

Yield: 12 to 36 servings.

Frijoles with Beer

1 1/4 cups (8 oz.) dry red or pinto beans
4 cups water
1/2 cup onion, chopped
1 (12 oz.) can beer
6 slices bacon
1 (8 oz.) can tomatoes, cut up
1 tablespoon snipped cilantro or parsley
1 teaspoon salt
1/2 teaspoon crushed red pepper

Soak beans overnight in 4 cups water. (Or in a saucepan, bring beans and water to boiling; simmer 2 minutes. Cover and let stand 1 hour.) Do not drain. Add onion and beer. Bring to boiling; cover and simmer for about 1 1/2 hours or until beans are tender.

Cook bacon until crisp; drain and crumble. Add bacon to bean mixture along with undrained tomatoes, cilantro or parsley, salt, and crushed red pepper; cover and simmer 30 minutes more.

Yield: 4 servings.

Zucchini Casserole

1/2 lb. bacon
1/2 cup onion, chopped
2 cups crushed crackers
1 teaspoon salt
1/2 teaspoon pepper
2 lb. zucchini, chopped
3 tomatoes, chopped
1 lb. sharp American cheese, shredded or sliced

Cook bacon in a large skillet until crisp. Cook onion in bacon drippings and drain grease. Combine cracker crumbs, salt and pepper. Lightly grease 13 x 9 x 2" baking dish. Layer zucchini, tomatoes, bacon-onion mixture, cracker crumbs and cheese. Repeat layers. Bake in preheated oven at 325 degrees F for 1 to 1 1/2 hours.

Yield: 4 servings.

Indian Corn Casserole

3 eggs, slightly beaten
1/4 cup flour
1 tablespoon sugar
2 (15.25 oz.) cans whole kernel corn
2 cups shredded cheese
10 slices bacon, cooked crisp and crumbled

Stir together eggs, flour and sugar; beat well. Add corn and cheese. Stir in three-fourths of the bacon. Pour into an ungreased 10x6x2" baking dish. Sprinkle remaining bacon over the top and bake in preheated oven at 350 degrees F for 30 minutes.

Yield: 4 to 6 servings.

Broccoli-Rice Casserole

2 cups quick-cooking rice
5 slices bacon
3/4 cup onion, chopped
1 (10 oz.) package frozen broccoli pieces, thawed and drained
1 (10.5 oz.) can of cream of mushroom soup
1 (16 oz.) jar cheese spread or cheese spread with jalapeno peppers

Prepare the rice according to package directions, except omit the salt; set aside. Cook bacon in a large skillet until crisp. Drain bacon on a paper towel, reserving 1 tablespoon of bacon drippings. Add onion to the skillet with bacon drippings and cook until tender. Crumble the bacon. Reserve 1/3 of the bacon for garnishing.

Combine cooked rice, broccoli, soup, cheese spread and bacon. Place in a 2 quart rectangular baking dish. Bake, covered, in preheated oven at 375 degrees F for 30 to 35 minutes or until heated through. Before serving, sprinkle the reserved bacon on top of the casserole.

Yield: 6 servings.

Texas Beans

3/4 cup brown sugar, packed
1/2 lb. bacon, cut up
1/4 cup onion, chopped
1 (15.5 oz.) can pork and beans
1 (15 oz.) can kidney beans, drained
1 (15.5 oz.) can lima beans
1/2 lb. hamburger, cooked
1/2 cup ketchup
1 teaspoon dry mustard
1 teaspoon salt
1/2 cup water

In a skillet, brown bacon until crisp. Spray a 2-quart casserole dish with non-stick cooking spray. Combine all ingredients together; pour into casserole dish. Bake in preheated oven at 350 degrees F for 90 minutes.

Yield: 8 servings.

Sweet Sour Green Beans

6 (14.5 oz.) cans cut green beans, drained
1 medium onion, chopped
6 slices bacon, diced
1 cup ketchup
3/4 cup brown sugar, packed

Combine all ingredients. Put in crock pot. Cook on high 4 hours, or bake in oven in a covered baking dish for 4 hours at 275 degrees F.

SMALLER PORTION: 1 can beans, drained, 1 slice bacon, cubed, 3 tablespoons ketchup, 3 tablespoons brown sugar, 1 small onion or 1 tablespoon onion flakes. Mix and bake for 2 hours at 250 degrees F.

Baked Stuffed Tomatoes

6 tomatoes
1/2 cup bacon, cooked and chopped
1/4 cup celery, chopped
1 small onion, minced
1 cup soft bread crumbs
1/2 teaspoon salt
1 cup shredded cheese
6 teaspoons butter

Wash tomatoes, but do not peel. Cut slice from top of each, scoop out centers and lightly salt inside. Combine tomato pulp, bacon, celery, onion, bread crumbs, salt and 1/2 of cheese. Fill tomato cavities with mixture. Cover with remaining cheese. Dot with butter. Place in greased muffin cups or greased baking dish. Bake in preheated oven at 350 degrees F for 30 minutes.

Yield: 6 servings.

New Mexico Refried Beans

3 strips thick-cut home-style bacon, cut into 1/2" squares
1/4 cup scallions
2 tablespoons minced garlic
2 cups pinto beans, with liquid
Salt and pepper to taste
1/2 cup grated Monterey Jack and Cheddar cheese combined

In a large skillet, cook bacon over medium heat until crisp, about 5 minutes. Drain on paper towels. Add scallions and garlic to skillet with bacon drippings and sauté over medium heat until they start to turn golden. Add beans with their liquid and stir to combine.

Toss and mash beans with potato masher or back of spoon until all liquid has been absorbed and beans are of uniform consistency. Add bacon and salt and pepper to taste. Transfer beans to medium-size serving bowl and top with shredded cheese.

Yield: 6 servings.

Wrapped Green Beans

4 (14.5 oz. each) cans whole green beans
1 lb. bacon
1 bottle Catalina salad dressing
1 can French fried onions

Make bundles of about 8 whole green beans. Wrap with a strip of bacon and tie securely. Place in baking dish and cover with Catalina dressing. Bake at 350 degrees F until bacon is done. Remove from heat and cover with fried onions. Bake until onions are golden brown.

Yield: 16 to 20 servings.

Mock Potato Bake

1 (16-oz.) package frozen cauliflower florets
2 tablespoons water
2 tablespoons butter
4 oz. cream cheese, softened
1 lb. bacon, crisp-cooked and crumbled or chopped
2 cups Cheddar cheese, shredded
2 tablespoons green onions, chopped

Place frozen cauliflower with water in a microwave-safe bowl. Microwave on High, covered, for 10 to 15 minutes or until very soft; drain. Place in an ovenproof 8x8-inch baking dish with butter and mash with a potato masher. Stir in cream cheese. Stir in bacon, cheese and green onions. Bake in preheated oven at 350 degrees F for 20 to 25 minutes or until brown and bubbly.

Yield: 9 servings.

Squash Medley

8 unpeeled yellow summer squash (about 1 lb.)
1/2 teaspoon salt
2 small tomatoes, peeled and chopped
1/2 small green bell pepper, chopped
1/4 cup green onions, sliced
1 cup chicken bouillon
4 slices bacon, cooked and crumbled
1/4 cup fine dry bread crumbs

Slice squash thinly and season with salt. In a slow cooker, arrange alternate layers of squash with tomatoes, bell pepper, and onions. Pour bouillon over. Top with bacon, then bread crumbs. Cover slow cooker and cook on low for 4 to 6 hours.

Yield: 5 to 6 servings.

New Year's Black-Eyed Peas

4 strips turkey bacon
1/4 cup onion, chopped
2 (10 oz. each) packages frozen black-eyed peas
1/2 cup brown rice, uncooked
2 1/2 cups water
1/2 teaspoon salt
1/2 teaspoon black pepper

Dice turkey bacon into a deep saucepan; add onion and sauté over medium heat until onion is tender. Add black-eyed peas, rice, water, salt and pepper. Cover and simmer over low heat about 45 minutes.

Yield: 8 servings.

Mushroom-Bacon Green Beans

4 slices bacon
1/2 lb. fresh mushrooms, sliced
1 medium onion, chopped
2 (14.5 oz. each) cans green beans, drained
1/8 teaspoon pepper

In a large skillet, cook bacon until crisp, drain; return 2 tablespoons bacon drippings to pan. Crumble bacon; set aside.

Add mushrooms and onion to drippings in skillet; sauté until onions are tender. Add green beans and pepper; cook over medium heat until hot. Spoon into serving dish; sprinkle with bacon.

Yield: 6 servings.

Baked Beans

1 gallon pork and beans
1 1/2 cups onion, chopped
3/4 cup green bell pepper, chopped
1/4 lb. brown sugar, packed
2 cups ketchup
1/4 cup prepared mustard
1 cup molasses
1/4 teaspoon chili powder
1/4 lb. bacon, cooked and chopped into 1/2" pieces
1 oz. cheese, shredded

Combine all ingredients. Place beans in a 9x13x2" greased baking dish. Bake in preheated oven at 350 degrees F for 45 minutes.

Yield: 25 servings.

Kentucky Fried Corn

6 strips bacon, cut into 1" pieces
1 medium onion, minced or in rings
4 ears corn, scraped from cob
2 small cucumbers, thinly sliced
1 large egg
1/2 teaspoon sugar
1/2 teaspoon salt
1/8 teaspoon pepper

Lightly cook bacon. Remove bacon; drain on paper towels. In a bowl, combine bacon, onion, corn, cucumbers, egg, sugar, salt, and pepper thoroughly; pour into remaining bacon drippings. Cook slowly so as not to brown too quickly, about 25 minutes.

Yield: 4 to 6 servings.

Side Dishes

Savannah Red Rice

6 slices bacon
1 cup onion, finely chopped
1/2 cup red bell pepper, seeded and finely chopped
1 cup uncooked white rice
1/8 teaspoon Tabasco sauce
1 teaspoon paprika
1 teaspoon sugar
1 teaspoon salt
1 cup canned tomatoes, drained and chopped
1 1/2 cups cold water

In a heavy skillet, cook bacon over medium heat until crisp and brown. Drain and crumble; set aside. Pour off all but 4 tablespoons of bacon drippings. Add onion and red pepper; cook over medium heat until onions are translucent. Add rice and stir. Add Tabasco, paprika, sugar, salt, tomatoes and water; bring to boil. Turn to low and simmer for 20 minutes; let set for 10 minutes. Sprinkle crumbled bacon on top.

Yield: 4 servings.

Crunchy Bacon Coleslaw

2/3 cup Miracle Whip salad dressing
1 tablespoon sugar
1/2 cup peanuts, chopped
4 cups green cabbage, shredded
1 cup red cabbage, shredded
4 slices bacon, crisply cooked and crumbled

In a large bowl, combine salad dressing and sugar in large bowl. Add peanuts, green and red cabbage and bacon; mix lightly. Refrigerate.

Yield: 8 to 10 servings.

Instant Wild Rice Stuffing

1 1/3 cups wild rice
4 strips bacon, diced
1/3 cup celery, chopped
1/3 cup onion, chopped
3 cups croutons
1 cup apple, diced
1/2 teaspoon salt
1/4 teaspoon sage
1/2 to 1 cup chicken bouillon

Prepare wild rice according to package directions. In a skillet, cook bacon over medium heat until crisp and brown; drain and set aside. Pour off all but 2 tablespoons bacon drippings.

Sauté celery and onion in drippings until tender. Combine rice, bacon, croutons, celery, onion, apple, salt and sage. Mix with a fork. Add chicken bouillon to desired moistness.

Place stuffing in a baking dish. Bake in a preheated oven at 350 degrees F for 30 to 45 minutes uncovered.

Yield: 2 to 4 servings.

Peppers and Grits

4 slices bacon
3/4 cup green bell pepper, chopped
1/2 cup red sweet pepper, chopped
1/2 cup onion, chopped
1 cup quick-cooking grits
1/4 teaspoon pepper
1/4 teaspoon paprika
2/3 cup chopped, peeled, and seeded tomato

In a large skillet, cook bacon over medium heat until crisp and brown. Drain and crumble; set aside. Pour off all but 2 tablespoons of bacon drippings in skillet. Add bell pepper, red pepper and onion to drippings. Cook about 2 minutes or until vegetables are crisp-tender.

Meanwhile, cook grits according to package directions; keep hot. Sprinkle pepper and paprika over vegetable mixture. Stir in hot grits. Add chopped tomato and bacon; toss to mix.

Yield: 6 servings.

Hoppin' John

4 slices bacon
3/4 cup onion, chopped
1/2 cup green bell pepper, finely chopped
1/3 cup celery, chopped
2 cloves garlic, minced
1 (15 oz.) can black-eyed peas, drained
1/2 cup beef broth
1/2 teaspoon dried thyme, crushed
1/2 teaspoon dried marjoram, crushed
1/8 teaspoon ground red pepper
2 cups cooked rice
1 medium tomato, cut in wedges, or 6 cherry tomatoes, halved
2 tablespoons green onion, thinly sliced

In a large skillet, cook bacon over medium heat until crisp and browned. Drain and crumble; set aside. Pour off all but 2 tablespoons of bacon drippings in skillet. Add onion, bell pepper, celery and garlic to reserved drippings. Cook until nearly tender. Stir in black-eyed peas, beef broth, thyme, marjoram, and red pepper. Add cooked rice; heat through. Garnish with bacon, tomato, and green onion.

Yield: 6 servings.

Spanish Rice

1/2 lb. bacon, chopped
1 small onion, chopped
1 small green bell pepper, chopped
1 (14.5 oz.) can diced tomatoes
1 cup uncooked rice
1 to 2 cups water
1 (4 oz.) can mushrooms, drained
Garlic salt, salt and pepper, to taste

In a large skillet, brown bacon, onion, and bell pepper. Drain bacon drippings. Add remaining ingredients and cook slowly for 35 to 40 minutes in an electric skillet at 275 degrees.

Yield: 2 servings.

Potatoes

Grilled Cheese Potatoes in Foil

3 large potatoes (pared, need not be peeled)
Salt and pepper
4 to 5 slices bacon, crisply cooked and crumbled
1 slice onion
1/2 lb. processed cheese (2 cups cubed)
1/2 cup margarine

Place all ingredients on heavy foil in the order above. Fold foil sealing all edges, leaving room for expansion. Grill for 1 hour, turning several times.

Yield: 4 servings.

"Sparkling" Potatoes

8 to 10 potatoes, washed
10 to 12 slices bacon
1 large onion, chopped
2 (12 oz. each) cans lemon-lime soft drink
1/4 teaspoon seasoned salt
Minced garlic

Wash potatoes and cut into slices (leaving skins on). In a skillet, cook bacon over medium heat until crisp and brown. Drain and crumble; set aside. Pour off all but 3 tablespoons bacon drippings. Add onion and cook over medium heat until onions are translucent.

Combine bacon and onion with potato slices in casserole dish. Sprinkle with seasoned salt and minced garlic. Pour 2 cans of lemon-lime soft drink over the potato mixture. Bake in preheated oven at 350 degrees F for 1 hour.

Yield: 8 servings.

Canadian Bacon Scallop

4 cups uncooked potatoes, diced
3 tablespoons flour
1 teaspoon salt
1/2 teaspoon celery seed
1/2 cup onion, chopped
2 cups Cheddar cheese
2 tablespoons butter
1 can French style green beans (drained)
8 to 12 slices Canadian bacon
3/4 cup milk
1 1/2 tablespoons ketchup
1/2 teaspoon tabasco sauce

Place 1/2 of the potatoes in a 2-quart casserole dish sprayed with non-stick cooking spray. Combine flour, salt and celery seed. Sprinkle 1/2 of flour mixture, onion and cheese over potatoes. Dot with 1/2 of the butter. Top with 1/2 beans and bacon. Repeat layer in same order. Combine milk, ketchup and tabasco sauce; pour over all. Cover and bake in preheated oven at 350 degrees F for 1 hour, then uncover and bake for 1/2 hour longer.

Yield: 4 servings.

Lithuanian Kugelis

7 or 8 potatoes (about 3 lb.)
1/2 cup butter
1/2 lb. bacon
1/2 small onion, finely diced
3 eggs
1/2 cup warm milk
1 teaspoon salt
1/2 teaspoon pepper
1/2 cup bread crumbs or cracker crumbs, crushed

Grate the potatoes into a large bowl that has been lined with a cheesecloth. Squeeze the juice out of the potatoes into the bowl and set the juice aside. Cut up bacon into 1/4 inch pieces and cook with onion until crisp. Remove from heat. Add butter.

In a large bowl, beat the eggs. Add potatoes, bacon mixture, milk, salt and pepper and enough of the bread crumbs to form a mushy mixture. Drain off the water that was the juice of the potatoes and keep the starch that settled in the bottom of the bowl. Add the starch to the potato mixture and mix well.

Spray a 9x13x2" baking dish with non-stick cooking spray. Pour entire mixture into baking dish and bake at 375 degrees F for 1/2 hour. Lower temperature to 350 degrees F and bake for another hour. It will be brown in color. Serve with sour cream or applesauce. Yield: 8 servings.

Bacon Tater Bites

1 package Ore-Ida tater tots
1 lb. bacon
Slices of American cheese, cut into three strips

Use 1 strip of bacon for every 2 tater tots you'll need as bites. Cut each piece of bacon in half and cook until lightly browned but still flexible.

Prepare the tater tots according to package directions.

Wrap a cheese strip around each tater tot, then the bacon around the cheese. Hold together with toothpicks. Broil, turning once, until bacon is crisp. Serve hot with mustard dipping sauce.

Mustard Dipping Sauce

1/2 cup mustard
1/2 teaspoon ginger
1/4 cup brown sugar

Combine all ingredients and serve with tater tots.

Layered Potato Casserole

4 to 6 baking potatoes
1/2 cup butter or margarine, sliced
1 onion, sliced
16 slices bacon
1 lb. shredded Cheddar cheese (divided)
Salt and pepper to taste

Wash and slice unpeeled potatoes. Spray a baking dish with non-stick cooking spray; layer potatoes, sliced butter or margarine, onion, bacon, most of the cheese, salt and pepper in dish. Layer until dish is full. Cover; bake in preheated oven for one hour at 350 degrees F or until potatoes are done. Uncover and top with cheese and bake until golden brown.

Optional additions: Broccoli, chicken, mushrooms.

Yield: 8 servings.

Scalloped Potatoes with Bacon and Cheese

1 garlic clove, peeled and halved lengthwise
4 lbs. Russet potatoes, peeled and quartered
6 oz. slab bacon, cut into 1x1/4x1/4-inch pieces
Salt and pepper
2 cups milk
1/2 cup heavy (whipping) cream
1/4 teaspoon celery seeds
2 oz. Swiss-type cheese, such as Gruyere
2 oz. sharp Cheddar cheese

Rub the garlic over the sides and bottom of an 8x12 inch baking dish. Steam the potatoes in a steamer basket over boiling water until they are nearly cooked through but still slightly firm in the center, about 15 minutes. Remove from the heat and allow to cool.

Sauté the bacon in a heavy skillet over medium-high heat about 8 minutes, just until it turns translucent and is beginning to turn golden-don't let it get crisp. Remove the bacon from bacon drippings, reserving both. Grate half the potatoes into the prepared baking dish, using the large holes of a standard grater. Season with salt and pepper, sprinkle with half the bacon and 2 teaspoons of the bacon fat, and repeat with the remaining potatoes, bacon, and another 2 teaspoons bacon fat.

Combine milk and cream, and pour over the potatoes. Sprinkle with celery seeds, then with both cheeses. Cover the dish with aluminum foil, and bake in preheated oven at 350 degrees F for 25 minutes. Remove the foil and continue baking until the cheese has melted and the potatoes are beginning to turn golden at the edges, 20 minutes. Remove from the oven, and let cool for 5 minutes before serving.

Yield: 6 to 8 servings.

Bacon Stuffed Potatoes

6 Idaho potatoes, skins pierced
9 slices bacon
1 1/2 cups onion, chopped
1/3 cup sour cream
2 large eggs, lightly beaten
Salt to taste
Pepper to taste

Bake potatoes in preheated oven at 425 degrees F for 1 hour. Cook bacon until very crisp. Reserve bacon drippings. Drain bacon and crumble in bowl. Sauté onions in reserved bacon drippings. Remove with slotted spoon and drain on paper towels. Add to bacon. Measure 3 tablespoons of remaining bacon fat. Add to bacon-onion mixture.

When potatoes are baked, cut thin slice from tops. Scoop out interiors, leaving 1/3-inch shell. Mash scooped-out potatoes. Add to bacon-onion mixture. Stir in sour cream, eggs, salt, and pepper. Beat until fluffy. Return mixture to shells, mounding slightly and smoothing with fork tines. When ready to serve reheat in 425 degrees F oven 15 to 20 minutes. Watching closely, broil 5 minutes to brown tops. Serve immediately.

Yield: 6 servings.

Potato Kugal

3 large potatoes, grated
3 eggs, lightly beaten
1 teaspoon salt
1/4 teaspoon baking powder
1 tablespoon cream
1/4 lb. bacon, cut in 1" pieces

Combine potatoes, eggs, salt, baking powder and cream. Pour in a greased 8x8" or 9x13x2" baking dish. Sprinkle bacon pieces on top and bake at 350 degrees F for one hour. Cut in squares to serve.

Yield: 4 servings.

Pasta

Spaghetti all'Amatriciana

1/2 lb. bacon, chopped
2 white onions, chopped
1/2 cup dry white wine
1 1/2 lbs. tomatoes, peeled and diced
1/2 teaspoon black pepper
1 lb. spaghetti, cooked and drained
1/2 cup grated pecorino cheese
1/2 cup grated Parmesan cheese

In a large skillet, cook bacon and onions over medium heat until browned but not crisp. Add wine, tomatoes and pepper; cook over medium heat until wine has evaporated and sauce has thickened. Spoon over individual dishes of hot spaghetti. Pass mixed cheeses at table.

Yield: 4 to 6 servings.

Quick Carbonara

8 bacon slices, cut in 1 inch pieces
1/2 cup whipping cream
1/2 teaspoon dried red pepper flakes
3 eggs, beaten
1 cup grated Parmesan cheese
1/2 lb. linguini or fettuccine, cooked
1/2 cup butter, melted
Salt and coarse ground pepper to taste

In a skillet, cook bacon over medium heat until crisp and brown. Remove from skillet, drain on paper towels. Reserve 1 tablespoon of drippings in skillet. Add cream and pepper flakes, heat until warm. In a separate bowl, whisk eggs and 1/2 cup Parmesan cheese. Drain pasta well, add butter, toss. Stir in egg and cream mixture, toss. Add bacon, salt and pepper, toss. Put in serving bowl, sprinkle with remaining 1/2 cup Parmesan cheese.

Yield: 3 to 4 servings.

German Skillet Pasta

1 1/4 cups uncooked, tri-colored, wagon wheel pasta
4 slices bacon, cut in 1" pieces
2 tablespoons sugar
1 tablespoon flour
1/8 teaspoon salt
1/8 teaspoon pepper
1 tablespoon country-style Dijon mustard
1/3 cup water
1/4 cup vinegar
1/2 cup celery, sliced in 1/4" pieces
1/4 cup onion, chopped
1 tablespoon fresh parsley, chopped

Cook pasta according to package directions. Meanwhile, in a 10-inch skillet, cook bacon for 2 to 3 minutes over medium-high heat or until crisp. Reduce heat to medium. Stir in sugar, flour, salt, pepper and mustard. Continue cooking, stirring constantly, for 1 minute. Add water and vinegar. Continue cooking, stirring constantly, until mixture just comes to a boil and thickens, 2 to 4 minutes. Stir in drained pasta, celery and onion. Continue cooking, stirring occasionally, until heated through, about 4 minutes. Sprinkle with parsley.

Yield: 2 to 3 servings.

Pasta Fagioli

1 lb. ditalini pasta (small, tubular pasta)
1 lb. bacon, chopped
12 cups water
1 (28 oz.) can tomato sauce
2 (16 oz. each) cans white navy beans with liquid
2 teaspoons salt
1 teaspoon pepper
1 1/2 teaspoons garlic powder
1 cup Romano cheese

Cook pasta until al dente; set aside. In a large skillet, brown bacon; do not drain. Add water, tomato sauce, navy beans, salt, pepper and garlic powder. Add Romano cheese. Heat through, add pasta, and bring to a simmer.

Yield: 6 servings.

Brie and Bacon Pasta

2 cups heavy cream
1 lb. linguine
1 lb. Brie cheese, rind removed and cubed
1/4 lb. bacon, crisply cooked and crumbled

Cook the cream, uncovered, in a heavy saucepan over medium heat until reduced by one-fourth. Cook the linguine in boiling salted water until just tender. Drain well and place in a heated serving bowl. Add the Brie to the hot cream and stir until the cheese is melted. Pour the cheese sauce over the hot pasta and toss to coat. Sprinkle with the bacon and toss again.

Yield: 8 servings.

Turos Csusza

8 slices of bacon, diced
1 lb. egg noodles
2 cups cottage cheese
1 cup sour cream

In a skillet, cook bacon over medium heat until crisp; crumble and set aside. Reserve drippings. Cook egg noodles until al dente; drain. Blend bacon drippings with the pasta.

Place in a large bowl and toss with half of the cottage cheese. Place in heated baking dish and cover with remaining cheese and the crisp bacon. Pour on the sour cream. Bake, in preheated oven, uncovered, at 400 degrees F for 10 minutes.

Yield: 6 servings.

Spaghetti with Bacon and Ham

1 (12 oz.) package spaghetti
3 tablespoons vegetable oil
3 tablespoons margarine
2 garlic cloves, minced
3 cups fully cooked ham, cubed
8 bacon strips, cooked and crumbled
2 tablespoons fresh parsley, minced
3/4 teaspoon salt
3/4 cup sliced ripe olives
1/2 cup grated Parmesan cheese

Cook spaghetti according to package directions. In a large skillet, cook vegetable oil, margarine and garlic over medium-high heat. Drain the spaghetti; add spaghetti, ham, bacon, parsley and salt to skillet. Cook and stir until heated through, about 3 minutes. Remove from heat and gently stir in olives and cheese.

Yield: 6 servings.

Desserts

Dark Chocolate Chunk Cookies

2 1/2 cups flour
1 teaspoon baking soda
1 teaspoon salt
1 cup butter, melted
1 3/4 cups sugar
2 eggs
1 teaspoon pure vanilla extract
2 cups dark chocolate chunks (break up candy bars)
1 cup bacon, cooked crisp and crumbled

Mix flour, baking soda, and salt in a bowl until well combined. In another bowl, cream butter with sugar until fluffy and light. Add eggs and vanilla; mix well. Stir in flour mixture. Stir in the chocolate chunks. Add bacon, stirring only until well mixed.

Using a cookie scoop, make large dough balls and place on cookie sheets lined with parchment paper. Bake in preheated oven at 375 degrees F for 8 to 10 minutes until golden around the edges.

Maple Bacon Treats

1 lb. bacon
1 package refrigerated crescent rolls
1/2 cup maple syrup
3/4 cup brown sugar

Spray a foil-lined cookie sheet with non-stick cooking spray. Unroll the crescent rolls so they are one single pane of dough; pinch any perforations together to seal. Stretch the dough out to cover the cookie sheet. With a fork, prick the dough all over. Set aside.

Cook bacon until just done; remove before bacon gets crispy. Drain on paper towels. Cut bacon into small pieces.

Drizzle 1/4 cup of maple syrup over dough. Sprinkle with 1/4 cup of brown sugar. Top with bacon. Drizzle the remaining maple syrup on top of bacon pieces, and add remaining brown sugar.

Bake in a preheated oven at 325 degrees F for 25 minutes or until caramelized and bubbly. Remove from oven and allow pan to cool before cutting or breaking into pieces. Serve slightly warmed or at room temperature.

Yield: 6 to 8 servings.

Bacon 'N Apple Muffins

1/4 cup sugar
2 cups flour
3/4 teaspoon salt
4 teaspoons baking powder
1/3 cup butter, melted
1 cup milk
1 egg, slightly beaten
1/2 cup apples, finely chopped
4 slices bacon, cooked crisp and crumbled

In a large bowl, combine sugar, flour, salt and baking powder. In a separate bowl, combine butter, milk and egg. Stir butter mixture into flour mixture, stirring just until dry ingredients are moistened. Fold in apple and bacon pieces. Fill paper lined or buttered muffin cups 2/3 full. Bake in preheated oven at 400 degrees F for 15 to 20 minutes or until done and browned.

Yield: 1 dozen muffins.

Caramel Bacon Bark

1 (14 oz.) bag caramels, unwrapped
1/2 cup sweetened condensed milk
1 (12 oz.) package chocolate chips
2 tablespoons butter
1/2 cup pecans or walnuts, chopped
1 lb. bacon, cooked crisp and crumbled

In a small saucepan, cook caramels and condensed milk over low heat for 10 minutes; stirring continuously until caramels are completely melted.

In a microwave-safe bowl, microwave chocolate chips in 30 second increments until melted. Add butter and mix well. Line a 15x10" baking sheet with parchment paper. Pour chocolate on the jelly roll pan evenly then sprinkle nuts and bacon pieces over the chocolate before it sets. Drizzle caramel mixture over top. Refrigerate until chocolate hardens, about 30 minutes. After hardening, break into pieces.

Chocolate Covered Bacon

Thick-sliced hickory sweet bacon
1 cup milk chocolate chips
1 cup semi-sweet chocolate chips
2 tablespoons vegetable oil

Place bacon, in whole strips, on a foil-lined baking pan. Bake in preheated oven at 400 degrees F for 25 to 30 minutes until crisp. (The bacon needs to be crisp but still pliable or it may break.) Remove and drain on paper towels until cool.

Combine semi-sweet chocolate chips and milk chocolate chips in a microwave-safe bowl. Add vegetable oil and stir. Microwave in 30 second increments on HIGH until melted. (If chocolate mixture seems too thick, thin it with a little more vegetable oil.) Dip bacon in chocolate or brush chocolate on bacon and lay on foil.

Bacon Pumpkin Bread

3 1/2 cups flour
1 teaspoon pumpkin pie spice
1 teaspoon ground cinnamon
1 teaspoon baking powder
1 teaspoon ground nutmeg
2 teaspoons baking soda
2 1/2 cups solid pack pumpkin
1 cup vegetable oil
2 1/2 cups sugar
3 eggs
1 cup raisins
1 cup bacon, cooked crisp and crumbled
1 cup walnuts, chopped

In a large bowl, combine flour, pumpkin pie spice, cinnamon, baking powder, nutmeg and baking soda; set aside. In a separate bowl, mix the pumpkin, oil, sugar and eggs. Beat with mixer until well blended. Add flour mixture and mix well. By hand, stir in the raisins, bacon and walnuts. Spray 2 loaf pans with non-stick cooking spray. Pour the batter in the 2 pans. Bake at 350 degrees F in a preheated oven for 50 to 55 minutes. Cool before glazing.

Glaze:
1 1/2 cups confectioner's sugar
1 teaspoon grated orange peel
6 teaspoons orange juice
Chopped walnuts
3 strips bacon, cooked crisp and crumbled

Combine confectioner's sugar, orange peel and orange juice in a bowl. Use spoon to pour glaze over the loaves, letting it run down the sides. Sprinkle walnuts and bacon on the loaf before glaze hardens.

Yield: 2 loaves.

Christmas Rum Balls

1 1/2 cups vanilla wafer crumbs
2 teaspoons cocoa
2 jiggers of rum, or enough to moisten the mixture
1 1/2 tablespoons of light corn syrup
1 cup confectioners' sugar
1 cup nuts, finely chopped
1/2 cup bacon, cooked crisp and crumbled

Combine vanilla wafer crumbs, cocoa, rum, corn syrup and confectioners' sugar; mix well. Roll the mixture into one inch balls. Combine nuts and bacon; roll balls in the nuts and bacon mixture.

Let the balls set in the refrigerator until slightly cooled.

Chocolate Truffles with Almond Bacon Centers

1 cup heavy (whipping) cream
1 (10 oz.) pkg. semi-sweet chocolate
3 tablespoons butter
1 1/4 cups toasted unblanched almonds, coarsely chopped
1 cup bacon, cooked crisp and crumbled

Heat whipping cream on medium heat until it just starts to boil. Remove from heat. Add chocolate and butter. Wisk until smooth. Cool to lukewarm. Stir in almonds and bacon. Refrigerate covered, stirring occasionally for 4 hours or overnight.

Take spoon and scrape across top to roll into balls. Freeze on baking sheet until hard. Melt chocolate chips or large Hershey bars over hot water. Dip candy in chocolate using spoon or toothpicks. Put on wax paper on baking sheet. Put in freezer or refrigerator until hard.

(Note: Leave the candy in the freezer and remove just a few at a time for dipping in the chocolate.)

Yield: 4 1/2 dozen

Maple Bacon Double Chocolate Cupcakes

3/4 cup vegetable oil
1 1/4 cups sugar
2 eggs
1 teaspoon vanilla extract
1 cup milk
1 3/4 cups all-purpose flour
1/2 cup unsweetened cocoa powder
1 teaspoon baking soda
1/2 teaspoon salt
1 3/4 cups mini semi-sweet chocolate chips
3/4 cup bacon, cooked crisp and crumbled

In a large bowl, beat vegetable oil and sugar until light and fluffy. Add eggs and vanilla; beat well. Add milk. Mix together flour, cocoa, baking soda and salt. Add flour mixture to sugar mixture; beat well. Add the chocolate chips and mix well. Gently fold in bacon.

Fill muffin cups that are lined with paper cupcake liners two-thirds full of batter. Bake in preheated oven at 375 degrees F for 20 to 25 minutes or until cupcake springs back when touched lightly in center. Cool on wire racks. Frost with maple frosting.

Yield: 24 cupcakes.

Maple frosting:

1 cup unsalted butter; room temperature
2 teaspoons pure vanilla extract
1/3 cup pure maple syrup; plus more for drizzling
1 teaspoon salt
1 lb. confectioners' sugar
1/4 cup bacon, cooked crisp and crumbled

Cream the butter with an electric or stand mixer. Add vanilla, maple syrup and salt; mix well. Add the sugar about a cup at a time and mix thoroughly after each addition. For thicker frosting add in a little more sugar. Garnish with chopped bacon and a drizzle of pure maple syrup if you wish.

Orange Pumpkin Cookies

2 1/2 cups flour
1/2 teaspoon salt
1/2 teaspoon baking soda
1 cup butter, softened
1 cup sugar
1/2 cup brown sugar, packed
1 1/4 cups solid pack pumpkin
1 egg
2 teaspoons orange juice
1 teaspoon grated orange peel
1/2 cup nuts, chopped

Combine flour, salt and baking soda in a medium bowl. In a separate bowl, beat butter, sugar and brown sugar until creamy. Add pumpkin, egg, orange juice and orange peel; mix well. Stir in flour mixture and nuts. Drop dough by rounded teaspoonfuls onto ungreased cookie sheets. Bake in preheated oven at 375 degrees F for 12 to 14 minutes. Spread cooled cookies with orange icing.

Orange Icing:
1 1/2 cups confectioners' sugar
1/2 teaspoon grated orange peel
1 to 3 teaspoons orange juice
6 slices bacon, cooked crisp and crumbled

Combine sugar and orange peel. Add orange juice, 1 tablespoon at a time, stirring until desired consistency. Frost cookies then sprinkle with bacon.

Cranberry Cake with Hot Butter Sauce

3 teaspoons butter, melted
1 cup sugar
1/2 cup evaporated milk
1/2 cup water
2 cups flour
1 teaspoon salt
1 teaspoon baking soda
2 cups raw cranberries

Combine butter, sugar, milk and water. Stir in flour, salt, baking soda and cranberries. Bake in an 8x8 inch pan for 30 to 40 minutes. Test doneness with toothpick. Serve with hot butter sauce.

Hot Butter Sauce:

1/2 cup butter
1 cup sugar
1 teaspoon vanilla
1/2 cup evaporated milk
6 slices bacon, cooked crisp and crumbled

Mix butter, sugar, vanilla and milk together in a saucepan. Over medium-high heat, bring to a boil. Pour over cranberry cake; top with bacon pieces.

Breakfast Bacon Cookies

1/2 cup butter, melted
3/4 cup sugar
1 egg
1/4 teaspoon baking soda
1 cup flour
10 slices of bacon, cooked crisp and crumbled
1/2 cup raisins
2 cups cornflakes

Mix butter and sugar together. Beat in egg. Add baking soda and flour; mix well. Stir bacon, raisins and cornflakes into the batter. Drop by rounded teaspoonfuls on an ungreased cookie sheet. Bake in preheated oven at 350 degrees F for 15 to 18 minutes or until lightly browned. Store leftovers in refrigerator.

Caramel Brownies

1 (18.25 oz.) package German chocolate cake mix
3/4 cup butter
1 (5 oz.) can evaporated milk
12 oz. chocolate chips
1 bag Kraft caramels
2 slices bacon, cooked crisp and crumbled

Combine cake mix, butter and 1/2 can evaporated milk. Put 1/2 of this mixture into 9x13 inch pan. Sprinkle chocolate chips on top. Bake in preheated oven at 350 degrees F for 6 minutes. Melt caramels. Mix with bacon and remaining milk. Pour evenly over baked mix. Add remaining mix. Bake 16 minutes more.

Candied Bacon

12 slices thick-cut bacon
1/2 cup brown sugar, packed
1 teaspoon ground cinnamon

Line a baking sheet with parchment paper or foil. Set a rack on top (like a cookie cooling rack). Spray the rack with non-stick cooking spray. In a bowl, combine sugar and cinnamon. Dip bacon in sugar mixture, coating both sides, and place bacon on rack.

Bake in preheated oven at 400 degrees F for 15 to 18 minutes, or until bacon is crispy. Check occasionally - sugar may burn if cooked too long.

Yield: 12 slices.

Peanut Butter Chip Cookies

1 cup brown sugar, packed
1 cup granulated sugar
1/2 cup peanut butter
2 eggs
2 teaspoons vanilla
2 1/2 cups flour
1 teaspoon salt
1 teaspoon baking soda
2 cups milk chocolate chips
8 slices of bacon, crisply cooked and crumbled or cut into pieces

Beat brown sugar, granulated sugar and peanut butter in a large bowl until light and fluffy. Stir in eggs and vanilla. Mix in flour, salt and baking soda. Stir in chocolate chips and bacon pieces. Drop by rounded teaspoonfuls on ungreased baking sheets. Bake in preheated oven at 350 degrees F for 10 to 12 minutes.

Pig and Monkey Bread

1/4 cup butter or margarine, melted
1/2 cup maple syrup
1 tablespoon ground cinnamon
1/2 cup brown sugar, packed
1/2 cup nuts, chopped
16 slices (1 lb.) bacon, crisply cooked and crumbled
1 can Pillsbury Grand's Flaky Biscuits

Spray a Bundt pan or 9" round baking pan with non-stick cooking spray. In a small mixing bowl, combine butter or margarine and maple syrup; set aside. In a separate bowl, combine cinnamon, brown sugar and nuts.

Coat the bottom of the pan with a little of the butter/syrup mixture; sprinkle a small portion of the cinnamon mixture on the butter mixture in pan and 1/3 of the crumbled bacon. Place biscuits in pan and top each one with the remainder of the butter mixture, cinnamon mixture and bacon. Bake in a preheated oven at 350 degrees F for 30 minutes.

Let stand for 10 minutes, then invert on serving plate.

White Chocolate Maple Bacon Fudge

24 oz. white chocolate chips
1 (14 oz.) can sweetened condensed milk
1/4 cup canned cream cheese frosting or 1/4 cup of butter at room temperature
2 tablespoons real maple syrup
3 slices of fully cooked bacon, crisply cooked and crumbled

In a medium microwave-safe bowl, melt white chocolate chips in microwave for 2 minutes or until melted, stirring every 30 seconds. Stir in milk, frosting or butter and maple syrup. Stir in bacon just until combined. Pour into an 8x8" or 9x9" buttered baking dish. Refrigerate for several hours until set. Keep refrigerated.

Yield: 24 servings.

Perfect Chocolate Cookies

1 cup flour
1 (14 oz.) can sweetened condensed milk
2 tablespoons butter
1 1/2 cups of semi-sweet chocolate chips
1 cup pecans
3/4 cup bacon, cooked crisp and crumbled

In a large bowl, combine flour and condensed milk. Melt butter and chocolate chips together in microwave for one minute or until melted completely. Add chocolate mixture and pecans to flour mixture; mix well. Add bacon pieces last and stir only until well mixed.

Drop on greased or parchment lined cookie sheet and flatten cookies a little. Bake exactly 10 minutes at 325 degrees F.

Peanut Butter Bacon Cookies

1 1/4 cups of peanut butter
3/4 cup brown sugar, packed
1 egg
1 teaspoon vanilla
1/2 teaspoon baking soda
1/2 cup semi-sweet chocolate chips
10 slices of bacon, cooked crisp and crumbled or cut into small pieces.

In a large bowl, combine peanut butter and brown sugar. Stir in egg, vanilla, baking soda and chocolate chips. Gently add most of the bacon pieces, reserving about 3 dozen pieces.

Use a cookie scoop to make small balls of dough. Place the reserved bacon pieces on top of the dough. Bake on ungreased cookie sheet in preheated oven at 350 degrees F for 7 minutes. Let cool before removing from cookie sheet.

Chocolate Pumpkin Bread

1/2 cup butter
1 cup sugar
2 eggs
1 3/4 cups flour
1/2 teaspoon salt
1/2 teaspoon nutmeg
1 teaspoon cinnamon
1 teaspoon pumpkin pie spice
1 teaspoon baking soda
1 1/2 cups canned pumpkin
3/4 cup chocolate chips
3/4 cup walnuts (divided)
1 cup bacon, cooked crisp and crumbled (divided)

In a large bowl, cream butter and sugar together. Blend in eggs and beat. Combine flour, salt, nutmeg, cinnamon, pumpkin pie spice and baking soda. Add dry ingredients alternately with pumpkin to the butter and sugar mixture. Mix in the chocolate chips, 1/2 cup of the nuts and 3/4 cup bacon. Grease the bottom of 9x5 inch loaf pan and pour batter in pan. Sprinkle remaining nuts and bacon on top. Bake in preheated oven at 350 degrees F for 65 to 70 minutes. Cool then drizzle with sugar glaze.

Sugar Glaze:

1/2 cup confectioners' sugar
1/8 teaspoon cinnamon
1/8 teaspoon nutmeg

1 to 2 tablespoons cream

Combine all glaze ingredients together, then microwave for about 20 seconds. Mix well, then drizzle on bread.

Yield: 1 loaf.

Mini-Loaves: This recipe will make 4 mini-loaves (fill pans 3/4 full with batter) baked for 40 to 45 minutes or until they pass the toothpick test.

Chocolate Bacon Bundt Cake

1 (15.25 oz.) box devil's food cake mix
1 (3.4 oz.) box instant chocolate pudding
1 cup sour cream
4 eggs
3/4 cup buttermilk or milk
2/3 cup vegetable oil
2 teaspoons vanilla extract
1 1/2 cups mini chocolate chips

In a large bowl, combine cake mix and pudding; stir well to remove any lumps. In a separate bowl, combine sour cream, eggs, buttermilk, vegetable oil and vanilla. Stir in cake mixture. Add chocolate chips; stir until well combined. Grease a Bundt pan well. Pour mixture into pan and spread evenly. Bake in preheated oven at 350 degrees F for 35 to 45 minutes or until an inserted knife comes out clean.

Chocolate Glaze:
1 1/2 cups confectioners' sugar
1/3 cup unsweetened cocoa powder
3 tablespoons butter, melted
2 to 4 tablespoons milk
6 to 8 strips of bacon, crisply cooked and crumbled

Combine confectioners' sugar, cocoa powder, butter and 2 tablespoons milk. Add more milk if needed to reach a consistency capable of pouring. Drizzle glaze over cooled cake and sprinkle bacon on top.

Nutty Sugary Bacon

8 slices thick cut hickory smoked bacon
1/3 cup brown sugar, packed
4 teaspoons spicy brown mustard
1/3 cup pecans, chopped

Place bacon, separated into strips, on a foil-lined baking sheet. Combine sugar and mustard; brush on bacon. Sprinkle with nuts. Bake in preheated oven at 400 degrees F for 16 to 18 minutes or until bacon is crisp. Cool for 2 minutes before removing from baking sheet.

Yield: 8 servings.

Bacon Brownies

1/4 lb. bacon, crisply cooked and crumbled or cut into pieces
1/2 cup margarine or butter, melted
1 cup brown sugar
1/4 cup granulated sugar
1 1/2 teaspoons vanilla extract
2 eggs, beaten
3/4 cup all-purpose flour
1/2 cup cocoa powder
1/2 teaspoon salt
1/2 cup chocolate chips

In a large bowl, combine margarine or butter, brown sugar, granulated sugar and vanilla; add eggs.

In a separate bowl, combine flour, cocoa powder, and salt; add to the sugar mixture. Stir in bacon and chocolate chips; pour into a greased 8-inch square baking dish. Bake in preheated oven at 350 degrees F for 25 to 35 minutes or until a toothpick inserted into the center comes out clean. Cool for 20 minutes before cutting.

Yield: 12 servings.

Salted Caramel Cookies

1/4 cup butter, softened
1 cup brown sugar, packed
1 1/2 eggs
1/4 teaspoon vanilla extract
1 3/4 cups all-purpose flour
1/2 teaspoon cream of tartar
1/4 teaspoon salt
1/4 teaspoon baking soda
2/3 cup walnuts, chopped
1/2 lb. bacon, crisply cooked and crumbled

In a large bowl, cream butter and brown sugar together until smooth. Beat in eggs; add vanilla. Combine flour, cream of tartar, salt and baking soda; stir into the creamed mixture. Add walnuts and bacon, stirring just until combined. Shape dough into a long roll about 2 inches in diameter. Wrap in waxed paper and refrigerate overnight.

Spray cookie sheets with non-stick cooking spray or line with parchment paper. Using a sharp knife, slice the roll of dough into 1/4 inch thick pieces. Place 2 inches apart on cookie sheets.

Bake at 350 degrees F in preheated oven for 10 to 12 minutes. Remove from cookie sheets to cool on wire racks.

Yield: 2 dozen.

Other Books by Bonnie Scott

4 Ingredient Cookbook: 150 Quick & Easy Timesaving Recipes

Slow Cooker Comfort Foods

150 Easy Classic Chicken Recipes

Grill It! 125 Easy Recipes

Soups, Sandwiches and Wraps

Simply Fleece

Fish & Game Cookbook

Cookie Indulgence: 150 Easy Cookie Recipes

Pies and Mini Pies

Holiday Recipes: 150 Easy Recipes and Gifts From Your Kitchen

CAMPING

100 Easy Camping Recipes

Camping Recipes: Foil Packet Cooking

IN JARS

100 Easy Recipes in Jars

100 More Easy Recipes in Jars

Desserts in Jars

All titles available in Paperback and Kindle versions at Amazon.com

Cover photo by Istockphoto

Made in the USA
Middletown, DE
22 February 2022

61708777R00102